ON 12 MAY 1999, Dr Winifred Ewing MSP, acting Presiding Officer, announced that 'the Scottish Parliament which adjourned on 25 March 1707, is hereby reconvened'. In the 20 years since then, we have had a further four Scottish Parliamentary elections. Five First Ministers and five Presiding Officers have been elected from an overall total of 306 MSPs, and of these 18 Members have served continuously. 347 bills have been introduced, of which 291 have been passed, 11 withdrawn, 31 have fallen and 14 are currently in progress. There have been 1,719 petitions lodged and 8,553 committee meetings held. 660 sessions of First Minister's Questions have taken place and 161,618 written questions have been submitted to Ministers.

Enric Miralles' vision for the Parliament building was for it to sit in the land among the people its Members represent. It is now firmly rooted.

# The Scottish Parliament at Twenty

Edited by
JIM JOHNSTON and JAMES MITCHELL

**Luath** Press Limited
EDINBURGH
www.luath.co.uk

First published 2019

ISBN: 978-1913025-33-5 (HBK)
ISBN: 978-1912147-98-4 (PBK)

The authors' right to be identified as authors of this book
under the Copyright, Designs and Patents Act 1988 has been asserted.

The paper used in this book is recyclable. It is made from low chlorine pulps
produced in a low energy, low emission manner from renewable forests.

Printed and bound by
Bell & Bain Ltd, Glasgow

Typeset in 11 point Sabon by Main Point Books, Edinburgh

Text © the contributors, 2019

Unless otherwise indicated, all diagrams are provided by SPICe.
'Open the Doors!' by Edwin Morgan reproduced with the permission of the Scottish
Parliamentary Corporate Body.

# Contents

Acknowledgements 7

Open the Doors!
EDWIN MORGAN 8

Foreword
KEN MACINTOSH MSP 11

Introduction
JIM JOHNSTON AND JAMES MITCHELL 13

1 Doing Right by the Common Weal
BERNARD PONSONBY 23

*Dear Scottish Parliament... Alicja Hertmanowska* 32

2 A Building Which is More Than a Building
GILLIAN BAXENDINE 33

*Dear Scottish Parliament...* 43

3 A Tale of Two Parliaments
LEE BRIDGES 44

4 The MSP's Role
ALAN CONVERY AND DAVID PARKER 54

*Dear Scottish Parliament... Claire Hossack* 64

5 Parliament and Business: An Unfulfilled Relationship?
MICHAEL CROW 65

*Dear Scottish Parliament... Dionne Hossack* 76

6 People-Powered Politics
FIONA DUNCAN 77

7 Local Government and the Scottish Parliament:
Parity of Esteem?
ALISON EVISON 89

*Dear Scottish Parliament... Ellie Gauld* 99

8 Scrutiny and Transparency
CAROLINE GARDNER 101

*Dear Scottish Parliament... Emma Cook*      112

9    Raising Taxes
CHARLOTTE BARBOUR AND MOIRA KELLY      113

10    Twenty Years of Devolution: Small Steps Towards Equality, But We Need Big Leaps
TALAT YAQOOB      127

*Dear Scottish Parliament... Etieno Essien*      136

11    Some Questions on Sovereignty and Free Speech
CHARLES ROBERT      137

*Dear Scottish Parliament... Ewan Carmichael*      149

12    A New Voice in the Land
JIM WALLACE      150

*Dear Scottish Parliament... Hope Teal*      160

13    The Role of Law
CHRISTINE O'NEILL      161

14    The Scottish Economy: Fiscal Challenges and Opportunities
GRAEME ROY AND DAVID EISER      170

*Dear Scottish Parliament... Quinn Muirhead*      180

15    Principles and Practices of the Good Parliament: Babyleave, Institutional Resistance and Change
SARAH CHILDS      181

*Dear Scottish Parliament... Robyn Gibson*      190

16    Look, Listen: This is Who We Are
JAMES ROBERTSON      191

Conclusion: The Scottish Parliament in a Changing World
JIM JOHNSTON AND JAMES MITCHELL      201

Appendix: A User's Guide to the Scottish Parliament
ELIZABETH CANTLIE AND ANDREW AITON      210

Contributor Biographies      219

# Acknowledgements

Our aim in this book is to take the opportunity, which the 20th anniversary of devolution provides, to reflect on the role of the Scottish Parliament and to look forward to the next 20 years, not least in terms of future challenges and opportunities. It is not an academic text and we asked all our contributors to write in an open and accessible style in keeping with the core principles of the Parliament. We thank them for doing so and also for their good humour and understanding during the editing process.

We would like to thank our advisory panel, consisting of Sarah Davidson, Christine O'Neill, Louise Macdonald, Sir George Reid, Caroline Gardner and chaired by Sir Paul Grice, who provided helpful advice on the content, purpose and contributors for the book. In particular, we are especially grateful to Louise for her proposal for a letter writing competition and to her team at YoungScot – led by Allan Lindsay – for running the competition. We thank all of the young people who took the time to write a letter and 11 of these have been included in the book, one anonymously.

Finally, we are indebted to our publishers, Luath Press and especially Gavin MacDougall and Carrie Hutchison, for their support, patience and encouragement.

*Jim Johnston and James Mitchell*
*May 2019*

# Open the Doors!

Open the doors! Light of the day, shine in; light of the mind, shine out!
We have a building which is more than a building.
There is a commerce between inner and outer,
between brightness and shadow,
between the world and those who
think about the world.
Is it not a mystery? The parts cohere, they come together
like petals of a flower, yet they also send their tongues
outward to feel and taste the teeming earth.
Did you want classic columns and predictable pediments? A
growl of old Gothic grandeur? A blissfully boring box?
Not here, no thanks! No icon, no IKEA, no iceberg, but
curves and caverns, nooks and niches, huddles and
heavens syncopations and surprises. Leave symmetry to the cemetery.
But bring together slate and stainless steel, black granite
and grey granite, seasoned oak and sycamore, concrete
blond and smooth as silk – the mix is almost alive –
it breathes and beckons – imperial marble it is not!

Come down the Mile, into the heart of the city, past the kirk
of St Giles and the closes and wynds of the noted ghosts of
history who drank their claret and fell down the steep
tenements stairs into the arms of link-boys but who wrote
and talked the starry Enlightenment of their days –
And before them the auld makars who tickled a Scottish king's
ear with melody and ribaldry and frank advice –
And when you are there, down there, in the midst of things,
not set upon an hill with your nose in the air,
This is where you know your parliament should be
And this is where it is, just here.

What do the people want of the place? They want it to be
filled with thinking persons as open and adventurous as its architecture.
A nest of fearties is what they do not want.
A symposium of procrastinators is what they do not want.
A phalanx of forelock-tuggers is what they do not want.
And perhaps above all the droopy mantra of 'it wizny me' is
what they do not want.
Dear friends, dear lawgivers, dear parliamentarians, you are
picking up a thread of pride and self-esteem that has been
almost but not quite, oh no not quite, not ever broken or forgotten.

When you convene you will be reconvening, with a sense of not
wholly the power, not yet wholly the power, but a good
sense of what was once in the honour of your grasp.
All right. Forget, or don't forget, the past. Trumpets and
robes are fine, but in the present and the future you will
need something more.
What is it? We, the people, cannot tell you yet, but you will know about it
when we do tell you.
We give you our consent to govern, don't pocket it and ride away.
We give you our deepest dearest wish to govern well, don't say we
have no mandate to be so bold.
We give you this great building, don't let your work and hope be other than
great when you enter and begin.
So now begin. Open the doors and begin.

*Edwin Morgan*

# Foreword

KEN MACINTOSH MSP, Presiding Officer

I HAVE NEVER forgotten the excitement, the optimism, or the sense of anticipation, which accompanied becoming a Member of the Scottish Parliament following those first elections in May 1999. Here was a brand-new institution that would help shape the modern Scotland and build a society of which we could all be proud.

I am pleased to say that, 20 years on, I have lost none of my hope, but I am conscious that, for my children, devolution is no novelty. They have never known this country without its own Parliament and, while I believe that what we have achieved in 20 years is quite remarkable, they are part of a whole generation for whom Holyrood is now simply accepted as the central focus for political and civic debate.

This timely book both looks back at the development of the Scottish Parliament over the last two decades and perceptively outlines some of the challenges that lie ahead. It does so, not as a dry academic textbook, but as an accessible collection of thoughts and observations. Jim Johnston and James Mitchell have pulled together a range of voices, from the winners of a letter writing competition organised by YoungScot to the more reflective comments of some of this country's most respected political commentators.

We share their journey, from the early ground-breaking legislation on land reform and the smoking ban, to the new choices thrown up by environmental and demographic change. The intervening years have seen some dramatic political ups and downs but, as the writer James Robertson remarks, the 'new political landscape looks remarkably mature after only 20 years'.

Devolution itself has changed considerably in that time and the Parliament is still wrestling with new powers over taxation and social security. Graeme Roy and David Eiser are amongst those who look to the potential risks ahead as we shape a new fiscal landscape. The Parliament still holds true to the principles of openness and equality on which we were founded but, as our own Gillian Baxendine writes, we have sometimes struggled to fulfil the promise to share power with the people of Scotland and to 'talk openly about the tensions between the representative democracy of the past and the growing demand for participation'.

On gender representation and diversity, in the way we use social media and encourage respectful dialogue and in the manner in which we establish trust in an era of fake news, there are plenty of political battles still to come. This book touches on all of those subjects and more. At a time when politics is often talked about with cynicism, it is a reminder that the Parliament still has the potential to fulfil all our hopes and dreams.

In the words of one of our young contributors, Alicja Hertmanowska:

I'm hoping for the best of the Scottish Parliament for the next 20 years and I'm very excited and looking forward to what the future brings.

# Introduction

JIM JOHNSTON AND JAMES MITCHELL

A PARLIAMENT HAS three main functions in a democracy: linking the people and law-makers; making laws and policies; and legitimising decisions. There are many different ways in which these functions can be performed. The Scottish Parliament was created with the intention of performing its functions differently from Westminster. It succeeded in being a modern, rather than a fundamentally different version of the House of Commons. The electoral system, hemispheric architecture, greater informality and serious efforts to fulfil its linkage function with the public were all built into the design. But the system of parliamentary government in which the Executive is chosen from within the legislature, and the Westminster experience of many leading members in its early years, ensured that the Scottish Parliament was part of the Westminster family of legislatures in its fundamentals.

The Parliament has become part of the everyday political furniture of Scottish politics. It is taken for granted – a sign of becoming legitimate in the eyes of politicians and the public. While debate continues on Scotland's constitutional status, few question whether the Scottish Parliament should exist. It is the focus of policy debates. Regardless of views on the merits – or demerits – of the policies or competence, the Executives emerging after each election have been accepted and have given Scotland the experience of almost the full range of possibilities: majority coalition, minority single party and majority single party. Relations between the Parliament and Executive have differed, but in each case, there has been no sense that the Executive lacks legitimacy. We have yet to see a minority coalition, but the Parliament is still young.

Parliamentary authorities took pride in their outreach efforts, acknowledging that links with the public needed to extend well beyond elections and the considerable efforts made by individual MSPs. Nearly five million individuals have visited the Parliament since 1999, as well as people from overseas seeking to learn from the Scottish experience. There was also pride in the early years that Holyrood was perceived to have stolen a march on the Commons in creating a modern Parliament.

But political institutions cannot stand still if they are to meet new challenges and take advantage of new opportunities. Not only must any legislature keep up with the times and respond to these changes, but it should attempt to anticipate change. As Lee Bridges, with the experience of working in both parliaments, states in his chapter, in relation to engagement activity, it is difficult to claim now that Holyrood is ahead of the Commons as a modern legislature. Reforms introduced in the Commons over the last 20 years have had a significant impact. Holyrood has considered some of the same reforms, including electing committee conveners; the Commission on Parliamentary Reform recommended that Parliament should put in place procedures for the election of conveners from the start of the next session, as had many commentators over the years. This recommendation is currently being considered by the Standards, Procedures and Public Appointments Committee.

Holyrood's policy-making potential remains under-developed. In large measure, this is a systemic problem and not due to any weakness on the part of MSPs. The 'Westminster model' is described as one in which the executive branch has considerable control over the legislative. This interpretation of both how the Commons and Holyrood operate can be exaggerated. Opposition members and government backbenchers can – and do – influence policy, but often in ways that attract little media attention and are hidden from view. Indeed, there is an inherent paradox in Holyrood, as in many legislatures. US President Woodrow Wilson had a distinguished academic career before entering politics and in one of his books wrote that:

> Congress in session is Congress on public exhibition whilst Congress in its committee-rooms is Congress at work.

That observation resonates almost two and a half centuries later. The Holyrood Chamber is the forum of much adversarial debate and it is in committee that much important work is done. But whether the committees have lived up to expectations is another matter. The recent Commission on Parliamentary Reform noted that

> while the committees have on occasion been robust in their scrutiny of government and others, overall, they have not been as effective as the CSG [Consultative Steering Group] anticipated in holding government to account.

Again, a point made repeatedly by a number of commentators.

Politics across the globe is contending with the need for greater transparency. This can encourage a more adversarial campaigning style of politics while ensuring that there is limited space for serious policy discussion which requires reaching reasoned discussion and consensus. The campaign mindset on public exhibition squeezes out the essential governing mindset required for serious policy-making. There had been much commentary on the 'new politics' which was hoped would accompany the establishment of the Parliament 20 years ago. It would be easy to dismiss this hope as naïve. Removing passion from politics is neither possible nor appealing, but Holyrood has struggled to cut out a significant role for itself as a policy-making institution. Holyrood has settled into the Westminster mould as an institution on exhibition. It will take a significant change in capacity, practices and behaviour of its members for Holyrood to become a serious policy-making institution.

The findings of the Budget Process Review Group illustrate the extent of this challenge. They found that there is little emphasis within the budget process on seeking to influence the formulation of the Scottish Government's spending proposals. It found that this was unsurprising given that parliamentary scrutiny of the budget began after the Government had set out firm and detailed spending proposals. Prior to that, there is little public consultation or transparency in the formulation of the budget. The group, therefore, recommended that committees carry out pre-budget scrutiny prior to the Government's publication of firm and detailed spending proposals and suggested this would require cultural change as well as changes to process and procedures.

Another area in which the Parliament has an opportunity to influence policy-making is through pre-legislative scrutiny. The Standards, Procedures and Public Appointments Committee concluded in 2015 that pre-legislative scrutiny has advantages and would give committees the chance to influence the development of a bill before it is introduced. The committee also recommended that all Scottish Government bills are published in draft. But, as noted by the Commission on Parliamentary Reform, committees have undertaken 'little pre- or post-legislative scrutiny'.

At the same time, as illustrated in this book, there is some evidence of committees effectively influencing policy development. For example, Jim Wallace recognises that he had to water-down proposals for a smacking ban and for raising the age of criminal responsibility in Scotland in response to committee scrutiny. Graeme Roy and David Eiser highlight the important role of the Finance Committee in influencing the structure and independence of the Scottish Fiscal Commission. The latter also point to the Economy, Jobs and Fair Work Committee's push to abolish pre-release access privileges for Scottish ministers for Scottish economic and fiscal data as a good test of the relative strength of parliament to force the government to respond to the will of msps.

The American Congress is the classic example of a legislature that has cut out a considerable policy-making role, including a role in budgetary matters. It lies at one end of the legislative policy-making spectrum of liberal democracies while Westminster-type legislatures lie at the opposite end. But Members of Congress have the time and capacity to scrutinise budgets in detail and to approve and amend spending plans. While there has been some effort to increase the resources of the Scottish Parliament, including the introduction of the Financial Scrutiny Unit, Holyrood still lacks the capacity of the House of Commons. The Scrutiny Unit in the Commons has significantly enhanced the Commons' resources in this respect.

But the linkage between parliament and government is not only about policy-making and scrutiny. Its oversight role includes agenda-setting. Members of the Scottish Parliament can set agendas by raising issues without necessarily having a ready-made policy and can push government to consider and develop policy. This is an area where the Parliament has made an impact, with members raising issues through questions and in debates in the Chamber.

## Increased Complexity

One of the fundamental challenges facing the Scottish Parliament is the increasing complexity of devolution. This compares to the relatively clear and intuitive nature of the original settlement. This was neatly summed up by Donald Dewar, as noted by James Robertson in his chapter, when he said in a speech in the House of Commons: 'Everything that is not reserved comes to Edinburgh'. It was never quite so simple. There was remarkable stability with few disputes between the two governments in Edinburgh and London regarding the powers of the Scottish Parliament. However, as devolved government evolved amid more challenging economic and fiscal times, it has become more complex with a much greater scope for dispute. As Christine O'Neill notes in her chapter, while

> devolution was never simple, I think it can be fairly argued that over the course of the last 20 years the task of understanding the boundaries of the Parliament's law-making powers has become progressively more difficult.

While the first ten years of devolution was relatively stable and the establishment of the Scottish Parliament was readily assisted by a favourable fiscal environment and relatively strong economic growth, the second ten years have been considerably more volatile constitutionally, economically and fiscally. The Parliament has faced considerable challenges in navigating waters which have become, simultaneously, increasingly choppy and muddy. At the same time, as the fiscal position has become much more challenging, the Scottish Parliament has taken on much greater responsibility for its own budget through significant new tax powers. This brings much greater risks, as well as opportunities.

Since the Scotland Act 1998, there have been two further pieces of legislation which devolve substantial further powers to the Scottish Parliament. The Scotland Act 2012 primarily implemented the recommendations of the Calman Commission including additional tax and borrowing powers. It also led to the establishment of Revenue Scotland – the tax authority responsible for the administration of Scotland's devolved taxes. The Scotland Act 2016 implemented the recommendations of the Smith Commission following the independence referendum in 2014, including further tax and borrowing powers and new welfare powers. As Graeme Roy and David Eiser point out in their chapter:

> The devolved fiscal landscape is now far more complex than it was in 1999, with new institutions and the transfer of much greater risks.

In a similar vein, Christine O'Neill emphasises the 'highly complex' nature of the devolution of the new social security powers.

The pace of constitutional change has again accelerated following the vote to leave the EU in the 2016 referendum. One of the consequences of the UK leaving the EU is the need to reflect on the robustness of the existing devolution arrangements. The first main test of these arrangements after the Brexit referendum was the introduction of the European Union (Withdrawal) Bill at Westminster. This was immediately viewed by the Welsh and Scottish Governments as a 'power grab' by the UK Government. The dispute rested on whether the devolved powers within EU competence should be returned to London, or Cardiff and Edinburgh, following Brexit.

The bill alters the legislative competence of the Scottish Parliament by removing the requirement for the Parliament to legislate compatibly with EU law. But it also alters the competence of the devolved parliaments and assemblies by introducing a new legislative constraint. Subsequent amendments to the bill and an accompanying inter-governmental agreement meant that the Welsh Government were able to recommend legislative consent for the bill to the National Assembly for Wales. However, the Scottish Government continues to have concerns regarding the constraint on the legislative and executive competence of the Scottish Parliament and the Scottish Government within the bill. While the Scottish Parliament voted to withhold consent the bill was nevertheless passed by Westminster, including this constraint, which as Christine O'Neill points out,

> empowers the UK Government, using secondary legislation, to prohibit the Scottish parliament from changing 'retained EU law'... in areas specified by the UK Government in regulations.

One of the key challenges for the Parliament is likely to be the extent to which the necessary revisions to devolution can be delivered through consensus and what happens if agreement cannot be reached between all of the UK's governments.

For the Parliament, this increasing complexity provides challenges in relation to all three of its main functions. First, in relation to the linking the people and law-makers, there is a need to provide clarity and understanding of the Parliament's new powers and how they work. Second, regarding making laws and policies, there is a risk – primarily arising from Brexit – that where laws and policies are made becomes increasingly contested between the devolved institutions and Westminster. Finally, the Parliament's role in legitimising decisions is likely to be tested by an increasing emphasis on inter-governmental negotiations and decision-making which will inevitably take place primarily in private. These challenges are discussed in more detail below.

## Linking the People and Law-Makers

As the constitutional arrangements across the UK become more complex and uncertain, there is a real challenge for the Parliament in how it fulfils its key function of both facilitating awareness and providing opportunities for public influence in its work. There is also a challenge, as highlighted by Christine O'Neill, in ensuring that both members and parliamentary officials have a good understanding of the evolving constitutional arrangements.

The Calman Commission's primary rationale for the devolution of further tax powers was to improve the financial accountability of the Scottish Parliament. This requires the Scottish public to understand the new tax powers. However, as Charlotte Barbour and Moira Kelly point out,

> a recent poll shows a lack of understanding among the general public as to which Parliament is responsible for specific tax policies [and] work is required in educating the public on the operation of Scottish taxes.

The devolution of significant further financial and welfare powers in the Scotland Act 2016 was accompanied by the introduction of the fiscal framework which sets out a complex set of rules and arrangements governing the interplay between the Scottish Parliament's powers to raise taxes and the block grant (the element of the devolved administrations' budget that comes directly from the UK Government). As each new tax is devolved, there is a reduction to the block grant equivalent to the tax revenues in Scotland which will now go directly to the Scottish Government. This initial reduction is then revised annually based on the relative growth of tax revenues in Scotland and the rest of the UK, adjusted for population growth. These calculations are not easy to follow as Graeme Roy and David Eiser highlight in their chapter,

> the parliament has had some limited success in bringing clarity to what is a much more complex set of budget arrangements, but there remains much work to be done to broaden public understanding.

At the same time as MSPs have had to develop their understanding of these complex budget arrangements, they have also had to grapple with the impact of Brexit on the devolution settlement. While all of the governments across the UK recognise that there will need to be revisions to the UK's constitutional arrangements, there are few details setting out how this will work. Despite this, the Parliament has begun to examine the impact of Brexit on its scrutiny role in relation to:

1. UK Ministers' use of delegated powers to legislate in devolved areas (previously within the competence of the EU);

2. The formulation, negotiation and agreement of international treaties, including trade deals which cover devolved areas, and which would previously have been negotiated by the EU;

3. Common UK frameworks which the UK Government and the Scottish and Welsh Governments agree will be needed post-Brexit.

As well as seeking to develop new processes and procedures to provide meaningful scrutiny in each of these areas, the Parliament also faces the challenge of facilitating wider public understanding and opportunities for engagement with the new areas of competence which will be devolved to Edinburgh following Brexit.

## Making Laws and Policies

One of the main advantages of the Scotland Act 1998 was that it was relatively easy to understand which powers were within the competence of the Scottish Parliament and those that were not were primarily set out in Schedule 5 to the Act. This meant that there were relatively few public disagreements between Edinburgh and London about where power lay within the new devolved settlement. There was little attention given to the constraints on the Scottish Parliament's powers arising from the UK's membership of the EU or other international treaties and agreements.

There was also little tension regarding the overlap between the devolved competences of the Scottish Parliament and the competences of the EU, even where this meant the UK legislating in devolved areas to meet the requirements of EU law, as it did often. It may well be that the likely constitutional arrangements which will be required following Brexit will work as smoothly but, at present, there is a real lack of clarity regarding what these will look like. There is also likely to be some disagreement between the devolved governments and the UK Government about where power lies in relation to the EU competences. For the Parliament, the key question will be the extent to which it will have the power to make laws and policies in areas currently within the competence of the EU and the extent to which there may be constraints on the use of these powers. For example, through the terms of international treaties agreed by the UK Government, including the future relationship with the EU. In some areas, there is likely to be the need for policy convergence across the UK but, in others, there will be opportunities for policy divergence. A key challenge for the Parliament will be to ensure there is openness and transparency in terms of the decision-making process for agreeing these future arrangements, including clarity regarding both the extent of the new powers and any constraints on their use, both legislative and non-legislative.

## Legitimising Decisions

This challenge is bound to be significant for the Parliament given the likely constitutional wrangling over where these powers will sit following Brexit. While there is a clear recognition within the Parliament of the need for a confidential space for governments to negotiate in private, there is equally a clear recognition of the need for effective scrutiny of any changes to the devolution settlement, including on a non-legislative basis. The experience of the process for negotiating the fiscal framework, which was subject to very little parliamentary or wider public scrutiny prior to its publication, demonstrates the difficulties in delivering this.

The extent to which decisions are taken at an inter-governmental level without scrutiny raises questions about the Parliament's role in providing legitimacy. If the only way to negotiate successfully and reach some kind of agreement requires a degree of private conversations, where does that leave Parliament? Legitimacy, in large part, results from the transparency of the decision-making process, levels of accountability and opportunities for influence within the process. This challenge confronts devolution regardless of which party is in government in London and in Edinburgh.

## Conclusion

As the Parliament enters its 21st year, it is clear that its foundations are secure and that it has strong levels of support as a representative body. But, as this book demonstrates, there is no room for complacency and the goodwill towards the Parliament is likely to be tested as MSPs of all political parties are faced with significant challenges over the next 20 years. In this introduction, we have highlighted that the increased complexity of devolution and constitutional change is likely to remain high on the political agenda. Other challenges, as emphasised by a number of contributors in this book, include the impact of a rapidly ageing population on public services and public finances. While there are new incentives for the Parliament to reap the benefit of strong economic growth in Scotland, relative to the rest of the UK, there are also risks if that growth is weaker, and this risk needs to be managed. This will require the Parliament to continue to evolve and develop if it is to fulfil its three fundamental roles of linking the people and law-makers, making laws and policies and legitimising decisions.

# CHAPTER I

# Doing Right by the Common Weal

BERNARD PONSONBY

I JULY 1999 was a brilliantly sunny day. I was perched on a raised platform at the top of the Mound in Edinburgh, anchoring STV's programme marking the opening of the Scottish Parliament. The day was memorable for the profound sense of celebration led by school children, politicians and ordinary citizens who jelled to forge a carnival atmosphere underscored by hope about the possibility of what might be.

That day, there was no Left and Right or Unionist and Nationalist. That day, perhaps uniquely in modern history, Scotland was as one in accepting that the new Parliament was a settled will that would become the focal point of national life.

The masterly speech made subsequently by the late Donald Dewar drew on his full appreciation of history, politics, culture and the sense of the place that the day would have in the nation's narrative.

'We are all fallible, we know that' he told MSPs,

> we will all make mistakes. But I hope, and I believe, we will never lose sight of what brought us here, the striving to do right by the people of Scotland, to respect their priorities, to better their lot and to contribute to the common weal.

His words were a declaration of ambition for the new Parliament and, what's more, a declaration no-one would possibly dispute.

Twenty years on and Scotland has changed. The Parliament has accelerated the move away from the douce, socially conservative and uptight feel of a post-war country dominated by deference to the monarchy, church and one's betters.

In recognising the rights of women, children and gay people, and by shining a light on the darkness of abuse whether it is domestic, sexual or sectarian, the Parliament has articulated a very clear sense of what is right and wrong. The rights conferred by the new institution, and its desire to better the lot of the less well-off, has perhaps been an unconscious attempt to define a modern notion of citizenship in which all are equal, and no-one is left behind.

It is worth remembering that Holyrood itself had to find its feet after a rocky, even tempestuous, start. The scandal of the Holyrood building project seemed to suggest that the new MSPs couldn't manage to oversee the building of a Parliament, never mind do anything useful with its powers. The spiralling costs led to Donald Dewar actively considering resignation after he discovered he had misled Parliament on the scale of the cost over-runs. As the subsequent Fraser inquiry made clear, there was no single villain in this story.

The narrative outlined in Lord Fraser's 2004 report would contain many salutary lessons for those seeking a better form of government. Dewar, it concluded, had been kept in the dark about much of the procurement process and given hopelessly optimistic assurances over the costs by senior civil servants which, in turn, he was passing onto Parliament.

The design competition was fatally flawed, potentially broke EU procurement rules and was executed by civil servants seemingly hopelessly out of their depth and areas of expertise. If you wanted to write a manual on how not to govern, then the Fraser report speaks volumes to a decision-making process which stood against the principles of openness, transparency and accountability. In some respects, given the timeline of the decision-making, this was the last bungled project of the government of the 'old' Scotland.

And then there was Dewar's untimely death. It was clear to friends that he was not enjoying the experience for which he had waited a lifetime. Cautious and measured by nature, motivated by the very best of intentions and high on social democratic principle, Donald Dewar did not find government easy. This was, in part, because he found it difficult to be a good butcher, to paraphrase Clement Attlee. He hated confrontation and did not deal with the jockeying that was taking place among his colleagues over who might eventually succeed him.

Henry McLeish's year in charge ended in resignation over an issue that should not have been a resigning matter, had he dealt with questions about the sub-let of a constituency office sooner. Initially, the right-wing press bombarded him with questions desperate to prove wrongdoing. Everyone else then joined in, convinced there must be something in the story given the ultra-defensive nature of the First Minister. Henry retreated to the bunker and, by the time he promised full disclosure over what he called 'a muddle not a fiddle', it was too late.

In the early days, the media did not so much scrutinise the Parliament as crucify it. Negativity and ridicule became irresistible themes and, in the issues of the Holyrood building project, the SQA exams fiasco, the errant behaviour of special advisers and the McLeish affair, they were presented with issues to give succour to Billy Connolly's acidic view that it was a 'wee pretendy parliament'.

Jack McConnell's legacy to the government of Scotland is that he steadied the ship at a time when it looked as if it could sink altogether. The media eventually, and not before time, wearied of the 'scandal narrative' it had championed for so long and got down to reporting policy.

What the early days of devolution proved was that little thought had been given to what a parliament would actually do. For decades, the agitation had been about the need for a parliament and then, in the run up to its creation, on crafting sound principles on which it should govern.

Whether the governments have been of the Scottish Labour-Lib Dem or SNP variety, all have operated in a comfort zone, rarely – if ever – taking unpopular decisions or seeking to face down a difficult issue. Devolved Scotland has proved adept at saying yes to spending money and a little reserved about initiating any debate about wealth creation upon which undoubtedly popular policies would be sustained.

There is a broad, but not unanimous, consensus around free university tuition fees, personal and nursing care, prescriptions and bus passes. Yes, there was initially the graduate endowment and Labour at one point looked as if it might back a different form of funding for higher education. But, by and large, it too operated in an arena of consensus with these policies. Skirmishes between the three broadly social democratic parties in the Parliament tend to be over the competence of government and not over policy ends.

The austerity years have put some distance between the SNP and its opponents on the centre-left over, in particular, funding for councils and further education. Again, these arguments are about spending priorities rather than irreconcilable ideological differences over the end game of public policy.

The basic organisation of the Scottish state has changed little in the 20 years of devolution, in part because politicians of the centre-left see the component parts of public provision as bastions to be defended and not altered. And, the vested interests which flow from that are rarely challenged.

The question about whether state provision provides the right service to the right people and what represents value for money is rarely posed. One Cabinet Secretary once told me that management consultants could find two billion pounds of wasteful expenditure in the Scottish budget without much difficulty. But rooting out spending that does not meet social democratic ends would offend someone at some point and, in a devolved Scotland, that is a path along which no government has decided to tread.

That is not to say that social democrats should be looking at private models of delivery but, rather, at whether the public provision meets the needs of the poorest sections of the community. Is policy sufficiently benchmarked against progressive ends or is it skewed to keep the government 'popular' and to manage the demands of vested interest ready to heap opprobrium via the 24-hour news cycle?

Post-war social democracy has rested on the building blocks of Keynesian economics, public intervention when the market fails and tax and spending policies to deliver greater equality. The unquenchable thirst for more money for public services has led to the various social democratic parties squabbling over who is the most progressive on taxation. And yet the relatively small yields provided by an extra penny on the basic and higher rates perhaps suggests that policies for economic growth would yield more than consistently resting on the 'more tax' mantra when a cash crisis hits the NHS or some other public service.

The new politics that Holyrood was supposed to herald in has failed to materialise. This is, in part, because tribalism has always trumped any notion of finding cross-party solutions in the national interest. The late David McLetchie said the essence of politics was conflict not consensus. That is true when it comes to left and right and yet the three parties of the centre-left have found little on which to make common cause because party interest has always come first.

Holyrood's 'yah boo' decibel level is not that much lower than Westminster's where, arguably, there are more profound differences in the parties that would, in part, justify the occasionally hysterical scenes in the House of Commons.

If there has been little serious thinking in the parties of the left, then the same can also be said of the Scottish Conservatives. The aforementioned McLetchie was a good deal more to the right than his clubbable image suggested. And yet he never really went after the left in the way of Michael Forsyth, with whom he shared many views. The Scottish Tories, for most of the period of devolution, have been cowed and have rarely led from the right.

Indeed, their recent revival was not as a result of any serious thinking about policy and strategy on their part. A section of the electorate, scunnered by the never-ending debate over independence, backed them in the wake of the referendum as the party most representative of their exasperation, not necessarily their values.

Thus, the revival has been fuelled by circumstance rather than sharp politics on their part. Independence paradoxically played well for the Scottish Tories as has Brexit. And with the SNP, Scottish Labour, the Scottish Greens and Scottish Lib Dems all trying to outdo one another on who is most progressive on taxation, the Scottish Tories' 'no to higher taxes' strategy has been authored for them. Rarely has an upward electoral trajectory been fuelled by so little hard thought.

The challenges of the next two decades are immense. The key hurdle to jump will be to sustain and improve the provision of public services which will be tested to the breaking point by a series of frightening demographic factors. Can the Scottish Government find the money to deliver what the public expects when the tax base looks horrifically narrow and where population growth is simply too marginal?

Two factors, it seems to me, need to be addressed – and quickly. Growing the Scottish economy is vital and there needs to be an end to the 'one-size-fits-all' Westminster immigration policy. The latter will have to change in Scotland, a country which needs more highly-skilled workers, if economic growth is to get to the requisite levels essential to sustain our current levels of public service provision.

The consequences of having to find lots more money in the future may be the crisis that jolts the Scottish body politic from its comfort zone, for politicians will have to think creatively to ensure public services remain sustainable.

In the early days of devolution, the Parliament benefitted from the UK Labour Government's massive spending programme through consequential increases to the block grant through the Barnett Formula. The explosion in Scottish Government income made social democracy look easy, since it was merely a matter of reaching into the pot to fund another worthwhile policy.

The austerity of the UK Conservative-Lib Dem coalition put key policies under pressure as there is now little room for political manoeuvre in harsher funding settlements. The SNP has, however, managed to sustain the gamut of 'free' policies. The opportunity cost has been that local government has continued to take a disproportionate hit of what Ministers call 'challenging settlements'.

On health, waiting time targets have improved over the last two decades, although the current Government is struggling to meet the demands of more ambitious targets. In the Scottish Labour-Lib Dem years, the SNP decried the Government's record. In the partisan world of payback, it is now the SNP who is in the dock. The fog of political war has clouded the fact that progress has been made, but that is the price an informed narrative pays to brutal tribalism masquerading as parliamentary accountability. All of the parties have been guilty of this at some point in the last two decades.

The challenges presented by social care in the future are enormous given a higher proportion of the population will be in retirement, living longer and likely to need some form of residential care if struck down by debilitating mental illness. The current system is already creaking at the seams, social care is yet another aspect of policy were the demands seem almost infinite but are having to be paid for out of a finite pot of public money.

The natural expectation, consistent with bettering the common weal, is that the public purse would pick up the tab, expanding even our existing expectations of 'cradle to grave' provision.

The sums involved in keeping 'free' policies free and asking the state to fund all long-term care costs are mind-bogglingly high. In the absence of new income streams, it is difficult to see how the Scottish Parliament will have the financial wherewithal to fund these and Holyrood will have to grapple with some difficult debates around funding. This is much in the same way as every other democracy in Western Europe where there is an expectation that the state will ride to the rescue of the infirm.

On education, closing the attainment gap is proving a challenge. The rocks have not yet melted in the sun and free tuition fees have remained – and look like they are remaining – so long as there is not a Scottish Conservative Government at Holyrood.

On areas of policy not tightly tied to expenditure, there has a been a mixed bag of results in my view. The smoking ban is now seen as non-controversial and an essential component of a sensible public health policy. The ban on fox hunting managed to see off charges of 'nanny state-ism' and the protracted fight to introduce a minimum unit price on alcohol may well pay dividends in the long-term. In all cases, it appears to this observer that they make sense.

The justice agenda has been problematic for the current government. The long and tortuous narrative on corroboration has been an example of how not to do good government: set up a committee (the Carloway Review) to recommend abolition, even if many members of the review panel wanted to keep it; continue to argue for it when the near unanimous weight of legal opinion is against abolition; dig in your heels as Parliament continues to question the wisdom of it; set up another review (the Bonomy Review) to dig you out of the hole you have created; and then let the issue sail into the distance. It was an exercise in political stubbornness, as was the introduction of the Offensive Behaviour at Football (Scotland) Bill, when it was clear that most of what was 'offensive' could be dealt with under existing law.

The one decision in the justice field that attracted the most comment firth of Scotia was Kenny MacAskill's decision to free the Lockerbie bomber on compassionate grounds. The easy decision would have been to keep Mr al-Megrahi in jail; no real fallout would have occurred from that and no-one would have kicked up much of a stink. And yet, if your system allows for compassionate release (and it should in a civilised country) and a prisoner is eligible to apply, it seems to me that the logic of the policy should take its course and not be torpedoed by populist considerations. The decision was courageous and, in my view, correct even if the medical reports on which the Justice Secretary based his decision proved inaccurate in terms of how long the convicted bomber would live.

The Parliament is owned by the people and, as a measure of how grounded it is, it is absurd to contemplate going back to the pre-devolution ways. On a good day, it articulates a sense of what kind of society it wants to create. When its members are at their most tribal, however, it depresses. It showcases the narrowness, often irrelevance, of the party 'bun-fighting'.

It has not been afraid to make different policy choices from Westminster and there has been little looking over the shoulder at what the older institution thinks best in policy terms. And yet the culture is curiously conservative. All of the parties have taken a safety-first approach to policy and rarely has the rhetoric of heady vision matched the reality of what has been delivered.

Scotland has been unquestionably improved but, in one respect, not fundamentally transformed by devolution. The existing levels of inter-generational, near institutional poverty are an affront to any notion of decency. That is not to say that Holyrood has not debated this issue at length, just that the challenges of breaking the connected cycles of unemployment, low incomes, poor housing, mental illness and substance dependency has proved a challenge too far.

Successive governments have demonstrated that they 'get' the issue; it is just that the whole business of government is sometimes defeated by the complexity and intensity of an issue. Lifting the marginalised from the fringes of our society to equip them to enjoy what most of us take for granted is, in my opinion, the biggest challenge facing our legislators. The issue is as much moral as it is economic and political.

All of our First Ministers have, in their different ways, been cautious politicians: Dewar gave the office gravitas; McLeish was here today and gone tomorrow; McConnell steadied the ship; Salmond reaffirmed the clout and standing of the office; and Sturgeon has proven highly-skilled in the business of governing. And yet, all of these social democrats have been high on managerialism, perhaps frustrated that, with limited powers, there is only so much they can do.

And, of course, the Parliament's powers have increased over the two decades. In Dewar's telling words, the creation of Scotland's Parliament was 'a process not an event'. Who knows where the next two decades will take us? In all likelihood, there will be another independence referendum; the only question would appear to be when and what event(s) will trigger it.

I want to finish with a plea as someone who has closely observed and seriously taken the journalistic discipline of holding politicians to account. Most of our politicians, most of the time, do a good job. Most are motivated by public service, not personal aggrandisement. In our system, we entrust the business of governing to fellow citizens, people who live and grow up right alongside us and who understand our community. The vitriol, mostly always uninformed, that seeks to deny the legitimacy of a point of view and which attempts to smear and denigrate, is the enemy of any democracy. The poison on social media confirms we have many bitter citizens but also many who are not at ease in the Scotland of today.

Perhaps the goal of the next two decades is to create a community called Scotland, at ease with itself and where everyone can disagree in an atmosphere of tolerance as our politicians strive to do right by those they serve.

*Dear Scottish Parliament...*

I think that you have achieved many great accomplishments. One of them being keeping this country stable and safe to live in, without any wars or political arguments with other countries. I do have some hopes and aspirations for the Parliament across the next 20 years and further future. My main hope is to let primary and secondary schools have at least one or two visits to the Scottish Parliament as I believe it is good for the relevant topics they may be learning about or just in general to have some more knowledge of the place and its workings. I have visited it before in Primary 7 for the topic of politics and found the experience very enjoyable and useful.

Another hope would be to keep the environment clean and safe for animals and wildlife especially if Scotland is known for its nature and forests. Even though this topic is spoken about often, I do believe that there is a lot of pollution going into this planet and I would be very proud as would many others if we could keep our country clean and for the Parliament to involve and encourage that more.

A further aspiration I think would be useful, and I know there are charities working towards fighting it, is to reduce the amount of people that are homeless and though that may be a difficult task I really believe that the Government and other generous and caring individuals will be able to help solve this problem and fight it for the new generations to come.

My last hope would be for the people who have lived in the UK for more than ten or 15 years and that were not born here, if they wanted to apply to be a UK resident then they would not have to hopefully pay as much as the price is now. I for example was not born here and moved here when I was one and a half, so I have been practically raised here but I am still not a UK resident and I'm planning on staying and would really like to be one since it is needed for a variety of jobs or certain events or surgeries and if the Scottish Parliament could change something about that I would be very grateful.

I'm hoping for the best of the Scottish Parliament for the next 20 years and I'm very excited and looking forward to what the future brings. Thank you.

*Alicja Hertmanowska, 15, Renfrewshire*

# CHAPTER 2

# A Building Which is More Than a Building

GILLIAN BAXENDINE

The natural amphitheatre will be the first form in the land. We hope that from this form emerges a series of identifications between the building and the land, between land and citizens, between citizens and building. Not just an 'image', but a physical representation of a participatory attitude to sit together – gathering.

Citizens sitting, resting, thinking, but in a similar place and position as Members of Parliament.

Enric Miralles, *Design Proposal for a Scottish Parliament*, 1999

THE HOLYROOD BUILDING was designed as a physical embodiment of the Parliament's founding principles of openness and accessibility. I want to explore three spaces where the building connects – or could connect – with its citizens.

The first is the external space. The way in which the building exists at the junction between the city (echoing the tenement gables of the High Street) and

sits in the land, because it belongs to the Scottish land; [...] to carve in the land the form of people gathering together.

(Design Proposal)

The second space is the building itself, despite the constraints of public safety and security. The citizens of Scotland were encouraged to regard it as *their* place, not solely the domain of politicians and the 'attentive publics' involved in politics, campaigning, law or journalism.

The third is the virtual space where much public discourse now happens. The constant appetite from digital space for images from physical space connects the digital space intensely to what is happening in the Parliament building. It also means, at least potentially, that many more voices can be part of parliament's debates.

## A Building Sitting in the Land

Space where the public can gather is part of a healthy politics. 100,000 signatures on a petition has weight but not as much as 100,000 people gathering in a space. And not just any space: one that reaches back into Scottish history – politics intertwined with place and landscape, from the seat of kings at Dunadd to the court of the Lords of the Isles at Loch Finlaggan. Enric Miralles also sketched the famous photograph of the St Kilda Parliament in the 1880s, collective democracy meeting every morning in the village street (albeit only for the men...). These things came together in the concept of the Moot (assemblies to decide issues of local importance), often gathering on a Moot Hill, of which a significant number are recorded in Scotland. Holyrood, however, is not above the landscape but nestled in it, down there, in the midst of things, / not set upon a hill with your nose in the air (from Edwin Morgan's poem for the building's opening).

The building and Holyrood Palace across the road embrace between them a new public space designed to encourage people to linger in the grass amphitheatre and around the reflecting pools. The doubters – it was too far from the centre of town; the Scottish weather was against it – have been proved comprehensively wrong. You might have expected the kids and dogs splashing in the pools on sunny days and the Parkour classes balancing along the walls to be chased off, but they have been treated as entitled to be there too. The space has been used for celebrations at key moments – like the Big Day Out at the start of last Parliamentary session with its music, dancing and families taking selfies in oversized deckchairs.

And it has consistently been used as a gathering place for protest or collective recognition. Pedal on Parliament; vigils around the independence referendum; the names of Scotland's First World War dead, a moving projection on the walls of parliament.

Once a symbolic space like this exists, it seems that people naturally use it week in and week out as a backdrop for the placards and photo-ops, calling on the Parliament to act on something that matters to someone in Scotland. Up the road, when we were in a cluster of temporary buildings, it was easier for the public to rub shoulders with members as they crossed the High Street back and forwards to the Chamber; still, members – including Minsters, who are in the building every sitting day too – regularly come outside to meet people advancing their claims outside.

## The Parliament is OPEN (or Tries to Be)

What we haven't wholly solved is how to draw people from the space outside to the space inside. The constraints of the site and of its security, especially the protective extra entry space judged necessary in recent years, means that this is not a building which, by its very shape, draws visitors in. The public coming down the Canongate pass two private passholder entrances before they reach the public way in, and increasingly large signage proclaiming the building OPEN has not offset a public entrance that looks rather closed. Security threats are real; of course, they are. Still, every so often the Parliament needs to challenge itself about how to welcome visitors so that their first moments in the building feel as little as possible like an airport. There is a real sense of awe and excitement for many first-time visitors to their Parliament and I hope that our current security review will consider if there are more ways, we can protect that feeling while whisking people through necessary checks.

Once inside, a great deal of thought went into making openness and accessibility real in the physical building. Free daily tours and talks; an easy-to-access visitors' restaurant and shop; a trailblazing free public crèche; a permanent Main Hall exhibition explaining the Parliament in easy to understand ways; and hugely varied temporary exhibitions, some, like the Great Tapestry of Scotland, draw huge crowds. In September 2018, the Parliament was awarded a 5-star visitor attraction rating from VisitScotland, affirming the original intention that the Holyrood building would be a magnet to visitors, irrespective of individual levels of political awareness and engagement. (We shouldn't over-emphasise the building as a magnet for *Scottish* visitors though; current best estimates are that well under half of the visitors coming in to tour the building are from Scotland.)

Public audiences are crucial to parliaments: MSPs need to know that they are watched doing their work and the public need to know that important decisions will be taken in public. This is why demonstrating our relevance and accessibility is one of the key strands in our Public Engagement Strategy. Unlike many legislatures, the public gallery in the Chamber feels quite close to the members on the floor and there is no glass between the public and the legislators. Similarly, in Committees, the front row is almost close enough to touch the witnesses giving evidence. While there needs to be a place for private discussion and negotiation, in the Scottish Parliament much of this also takes place in and around the beautiful central Garden Lobby where staff, journalists and members are continually passing and repassing each other. The recent introduction of a Lobbying Register is another important step to bring more of what happens behind the scenes into public daylight.

The public cannot just be an audience, though. Every week hundreds of people come into the Parliament for events, receptions and Cross-Party Groups, filling committee rooms and the Garden Lobby to campaign for changes and celebrate achievements with their elected members. More radically, from time to time the spaces are completely taken over with palm trees, tartan sofas and jazz bands for the Festival of Politics when as far as possible people are free to wander the spaces, debating and discussing topics of the day. At other times the Scottish Youth Parliament, International Women's Day or the Business in the Parliament Conference take over members' seats in the Chamber to debate their own priorities.

## Participants, Not Just Audiences

These events are still at the edges of Parliament. What about the public as participants in the real business of parliament? This is the second strand of our Public Engagement Strategy – real public influence on issues of concern.

There is the public petitions system which allows and – an advantage of a small country – supports even a single signatory to have their petition assessed and, where appropriate, pursued with government. It's easy to forget how innovative this was in 1999, and it has become a model that other countries have looked to. Research has emphasised that the process of petitioning is almost as important as the outcome: people who have had a fair hearing will still feel that it was worthwhile, even if they don't get what they wanted. But petitioners are overwhelmingly male, white and older, rather like the general pattern of witnesses who appear in front of committees; and even so the system is bending under the weight of petitions. If we are successful in widening the pool of petitioners, we also need to recognise that the petitions system will take up more resources – or that more conditions will need to be set on petitions, as happens in other systems.

Petitions are powerful but they can't be the only route. Scottish

Parliament committees have always prioritised public engagement and it has been satisfying to see how the devolved legislatures have challenged the House of Commons to be more ambitious. Initially there was more of a line drawn between the kind of people who would be comfortable in a formal committee meeting and those committees met out in communities on many visits and at events. Some people don't want to tell their experiences on camera at the daunting end of a huge table. They may not be confident, or their story may be too personal, or they simply don't have the time, money or health to travel to Edinburgh. It's important for the Parliament to be visible in communities and some things can only be properly understood by going to see them.

However, we underestimated at first who might be ready to take part in proceedings. A turning point was the Welfare Reform Committee's Your Say initiative which sought out the stories of people with first-hand experience of the benefits system. At first people were encouraged to write in but the passion and frustration in their accounts seemed to demand more. Individuals were visited in their own homes or communities for a cup of tea and a chat with a committee clerk, to explore whether they wanted to tell their story to the Committee in public, on camera, in a committee meeting. Many did and it was clear that what was important to them was precisely that their experiences would become part of the public record, be heard face-to-face by members and by the press. Since then many other people have, with care and support, sat at the table: primary school children, gypsy-travellers, people with experience of homelessness, care-experienced young people, modern apprentices. (There is a lovely recent Instagram story showing two construction apprentices skipping out of the committee room grinning and telling anyone who gets the chance to take up the opportunity to speak to a committee.)

Related to this, hundreds of school children take part in Parliamentary education sessions every year. We used to use illustrative issues to show them how Parliament works but increasingly we are using live committee consultations where the views from the sessions will be fed straight into Parliamentary business.

We go to many conferences and events every year. Rather than just tell people about the Parliament we are starting to take out 'pop-up democracy' – live surveys and consultations. For example, one of my colleagues recently spent an afternoon at Kwik Fit in Dunfermline, asking customer's views on the 20mph Speed Limit Bill.

The next stage is to get better at telling people what happens next – moving on from 'drive-by consultation' – by making sure that we tell people who've been involved what happened as a result. What did the committee recommend? How did the government respond? What happens next? That also challenges us to evaluate our public engagement better: is it actually making a difference to the committees' thinking? Because, if not, people will certainly tire of giving up their time to speak to us.

## More Than Just Witnesses: Deliberative Democracy

It's clear that we haven't exhausted the potential to involve people in committee meetings and community visits but there are also more radical approaches to be tried. Citizens' juries and assemblies are beginning to be part of the consultation landscape in Scotland, not only in the Parliament but in national and local government. This thinking reflects emerging international practice around what is often called deliberation– a way of thinking about democracy that emphasises not just the decision-making moment, but all the processes of opinion formation and public debating that go on before matters come to a vote.

Claudia Chwalisz, who has researched this approach extensively in recent years writes:

> The benefits of political leaders and civil servants engaging in participatory governance are well documented. Across fields as diverse as education, health care, infrastructure development and environmental protection…, an approach which engages citizens directly in the decision-making process leads to faster responses to problems, more effective design and development of appropriate solutions, and higher levels of commitment and motivation to implement the programme. Importantly, there are also higher levels of public satisfaction with policies that have been developed in a participatory way.

While most deliberative events in the UK have either been initiated outside of government or contracted out by government, uniquely (I believe) the Scottish Parliament has established its own in-house unit to develop the skills and capacity to run this type of event for committees. By the time this is published the first citizens' jury will have met in the Scottish

Parliament, based on a belief that an informed public is more than capable of weighing up the balances and trade-offs inherent in democratic decision-making. Potentially, decisions made by such methods have more legitimacy and more enduring public backing for hard choices, as has been demonstrated in the Republic of Ireland.

Because these 'mini-publics' are randomly selected, and a thank-you payment is made for their time as well as expenses met, in theory any adult in Scotland could take part. At the very least, the panel coming in in March includes people from every age group, educational background and region of Scotland and so looks nothing like the usual committee witnesses. Many of them will never have been involved in formal politics.

These approaches are expensive and time-consuming. We are still working out what questions they should be used for and we have yet to see how committees will use and value their findings or how members will negotiate the sometimes-uneasy border between representative and participatory democracy. For the right questions, they offer exciting possibilities of signalling that anyone can be supported to become a thoughtful political participant. And we think the symbolism of coming into the building is part of the attraction: the invitation we sent out began 'How would you like to spend a weekend at the Scottish Parliament?'.

A different model is the Young Women Lead committee, a partnership with a third sector organisation, the Young Women's Movement. Young women are under-represented and under-involved in politics and we wanted a way of building up their confidence to have a voice in public debate. This project gives 30 young women their own Parliamentary committee, with a clerk, research support, social media and press training, and Deputy Presiding Officer Linda Fabiani MSP as their Convener.

Last year's committee chose its own topic – sexual harassment in schools – on which it took evidence from external and Scottish Government witnesses, engaged with other young women in communities and produced a report. Many people commented on the focus of their questioning and the succinct clarity of their report (something for Parliamentary committees to learn from?). We hadn't been sure what would happen to the report, but it was subsequently considered by the MSPs on the Equalities and Human Rights Committee, who questioned the Deputy First Minister on its recommendations and made sure that he provided a formal response as for any other Parliamentary report. This year's committee are looking at young women's participation in physical activity;

meanwhile we are exploring whether there are other under-represented groups who might use a similar model.

Young Women Lead was an example where the Parliament wasn't setting the agenda of the discussion. Committees have experimented a little with this – asking people to suggest topics for inquiry or questions for ministers. This year as part of our 20th anniversary programme we hope to take this further by going into communities – particularly ones with low voter registration and low engagement with the Parliament generally – and working with people in those communities to define their own agenda and priorities. We don't know quite what this will look like yet except that it will be different from the Parliament turning up to talk about what *we* want to talk about at some version of a town hall meeting.

These kinds of participation are about something fundamental: reversing some of the distance between 'high politics' and people's day-to-day experience of political issues and public services which, at worst, can breed a sense of detachment and cynicism. Survey data suggests that trust in governance in Scotland remains higher than in other parts of the UK, but at times of political uncertainty and upheaval as well as social and demographic changes, it becomes even more important that people do not feel that their voices are excluded from discussions about the important matters in all our lives.

## Participation in the Digital Space

All these activities are rooted in the Parliament building but how relevant does physical space remain in a digital world?

John Parkinson (in *Democracy and Public Space*) highlights the way that digital spaces are in fact hungry for images and stories from the physical world. Social media and online news sites want pictures of people gathering, talking, doing things which they can take and share. I mentioned the diverse sorts of people increasingly giving evidence to committees: social media can amplify this so that several thousand more people can see who is being given a voice in parliament. Twitter, blogs and YouTube remove many of the barriers for people to become commentators, not just observers, on the political arena.

Digital forums also, potentially, allow people to talk directly to each other to develop ideas, not just on a single channel between themselves and the Parliament. This is not a tool the Parliament is yet skilled at using, and there are challenges in turning this more scattered and piecemeal evidence into something committees know how to use in scrutiny. Policy can't be based on single stories however powerful or heart-breaking, but stories bring issues alive and illuminate the questions that need to be asked and strengthen the will to ask those questions: Is this acceptable? Is it happening to other people? Can it be made better? Digital spaces can also then bring more voices into generating and testing solutions.

Digital tools also allow more people to take part, and at a distance or at their convenience. Early career academics rarely have a travel budget or a day free from teaching commitments but from this year, we will be able to Skype them – or anyone else – into a committee meeting from their laptop in their own home or office. 360° immersive video of the building allows anyone in Scotland to walk around their Parliament and lets potential witnesses 'sit' at the end of a committee table and really feel what it will be like when they walk into that room and face questioning by members.

However, we know all too well that the absence of strong social connections in digital space feeds the incivility of online debate. 'Trust and empathy require a human touch' (Chwalisz) and the performance of democracy requires anchoring in a physical place, as well as in procedures which give at least some dignity and boundaries to political debate. The building's designers may have been over-optimistic about the power of a horseshoe chamber to create consensus, but the sense of walking onto a significant stage in the Chamber or committee is part of what cues the behaviour of both members and public, cues that are missing from most of the digital world.

## Something More?

Our democracy may at times tend towards consensus and at others towards sharp division; but neither consensus nor conflict guarantees a wide diversity of opinion. Let alone space for the ideas of the future whose time has not yet come. We need to keep challenging ourselves relentlessly, noticing how easy it is for our events to become routine and unimaginative or for limitations such as the need for physical security to be taken for granted rather than pushed. We need, both members and staff, to be unafraid to talk openly about the tensions between the representative democracy of the past and the growing demand for participation and how we can experiment with blending the two.

Each decade, our population is becoming older, better educated and better off. That means we have more and more people who feel well-equipped to take part in democratic decision-making and more impatient when they aren't included. It also means a significant group of people who – because they are younger or poorer or less educated – feel left out and left behind. Our challenge is to keep innovating and experimenting for and with all of them. Or to quote Edwin Morgan again:

> in the present and the future you will
> need something more.
> What is it? We, the people, cannot tell you yet, but you will know
> about it when we do tell you.

*Dear Scottish Parliament...*

I want to express my hopes for a better process for dealing with bullying and cyber bullying.

I myself have and still am being bullied at school and I am in S3. The issues I have experienced are mainly verbal but are physical roughly one third of the time.

The way the amazing teachers at my school could be taught about how to deal with bullying in general is that they should all have to go on a training course which tells them all the signs and how to punish people who are bullying others. If this training is created and carried out across the United Kingdom it would help children like me feel like we can relax, make friends, work better and be less stressed.

The way this would help the Parliament is that people who are bullied won't be anymore and won't need counselling or a tutor which uses money which the school or parents don't have.

Personally, if this issue is sorted it would aid me greatly and let me work more confidently and be less shy to ask other people around me and the teacher for help or answers. I will also be able to feel more welcome and fit in better with my peers (other pupils). Hopefully this problem gets resolved and all the other pupils who get bullied including me feel better about coming to school and mostly feeling safe everywhere at any time.

[If you are being bullied, know someone who is being bullied or would like information on how to respond to bullying, please visit www.young.scot/bullying.]

CHAPTER 3

# A Tale of Two Parliaments

LEE BRIDGES

*Please raise your right hand and repeat after me… I, George Newlands
Reid, do swear that I will be faithful and bear true allegiance…*

ON 7 MAY 2003 I found myself standing in the well of the Chamber with the
terrifying honour of administering the oath and affirmations to new Members of the Scottish Parliament. It was the beginning of the second session of
the new Parliament and I didn't know for sure that the person I was swearing in at that moment would become our second Presiding Officer, and I
certainly didn't know at that point that I would soon become his Principal
Private Secretary and have four years of adventures ahead of me.

Sixteen and a bit years after that swearing in, I was in the Officials
Box in the House of Commons Chamber watching the Leader of the
House introduce proposals for an independent complaints and grievance
scheme for the UK Parliament. I had the similarly terrifying honour of
being the Senior Responsible Owner for delivering the scheme. This was
ground-breaking stuff and had taken a huge team effort of colleagues
and expert advisers to draw together a system of investigation and sanctions intended to begin to change the culture at Westminster.

What follows is a personal view of what I have experienced in those
two legislatures and therefore my reflections may not be shared by people who were also there at the time. That is fine, as this chapter is not
intended to be the unassailable truth of what happened, merely one view
intended to provoke others to reflect. I am still employed by the Commons and have a lot of good friends at the Scottish Parliament, so this
will not be a scandalous kiss-and-tell account of life in the black and
white or green-carpeted corridors of power. Rather, I want to focus on
the people who are employed by these two parliaments and the emotion
that drives them in supporting democracy. There are plenty of accounts
of what has happened over the past 20 years, what those events have
meant to process, policy, procedure or individuals. What I am aiming

to do is to fill a bit of a gap in the market and concentrate on how those things *felt* to those of us working in those democratic institutions and how this emotional impact shaped us in shaping them.

# Part 1: Holyrood

It began for me on a dreich Monday in March 1999 when I joined a small but perfectly-formed group of parliamentary clerks in Saughton House in the west of Edinburgh. On first impressions, Saughton House was stark from the outside and strangely laid out into 'spurs' inside. For a flat-vowelled Grimsby boy, the first challenge started with people not really knowing what I was talking about when I said I was working in 'sorton' and to this day I can't get my throat to give it its proper pronunciation 'sockton'. Environment and accent aside, this rather unpromising building contained the fledgling parliamentary staff who were working hard to bring to life all the components of a modern, effective legislature.

It was a wonderful and exciting time – we basically had two source materials, and our imaginations, to work with. The Scotland Act 1998 was the legislation that brought the Scottish Parliament into being, and the regulations made from that gave us the legislative framework. Then there was the report from the Consultative Steering Group (CSG) which had brought together people from all parts of civic society to provide a blueprint for how the Parliament should operate, what is should hold dear and set out the high expectations that the people of Scotland had for it. Time and tide may have dimmed the radicalism of this report, but in late 20th century Britain it enthused and terrified us in equal measure. This report leads me to my first pondering.

At the heart of the CSG's aspirational directions to us putting the Parliament together were the four principles:

the Scottish Parliament should embody and reflect the sharing of power between the people of Scotland, the legislators and the Scottish Executive;

the Scottish Executive should be accountable to the Scottish Parliament and the Parliament and Executive should be accountable to the people of Scotland;

the Scottish Parliament should be accessible, open, responsive and develop procedures which make possible a participative approach to the development, consideration and scrutiny of policy and legislation;

the Scottish Parliament in its operation and its appointments should recognise the need to promote equal opportunities for all.

To a small group of fresh and enthusiastic officials under considerable time pressure to get a legislature up and running in the midst of the first Scottish general election campaign, these principles were manna from heaven. Not only did they help us in practical ways when drafting committee procedures or pushing us to make sure that we concentrated on a dedicated visitor centre (a radical thing back then) it also made us feel that we were on a bigger mission. The commitment to the people, to promoting equality of opportunity and the reinterpretation of representative democracy through sharing power made me feel, as one small part of that mission, that I was doing something big and it spoke loudly to my sense of public service.

I am too cowardly to be a fire-fighter, too squeamish to be a nurse and too thin-skinned to stand for elected office – but here I was in the vanguard of a great change to the way people thought about politics, with an understanding that we could be better, the country could be better and that democracy was about to move to a whole new level. It is hard to articulate what this meant personally to me, but I felt it in my stomach and it made me excited to go to work, to work hard when I got there and talk exuberantly about my day when me and my new friends went to the pub in the evening. I know, I know – rose-tinted glasses and all that and it certainly wasn't all blue-sky, utopia-building.

One particularly long, excruciating email discussion one wet Friday afternoon about the relative merits of using treasury tags or paper clips for committee papers was a prick in that high-minded bubble. But there was something special about that time and my first recommendation, well challenge really, is to say that the CSG report is well worth re-reading. For my cohort of colleagues, many of whom are still there, my question is are those four principles still inspiring the way you do your jobs? Would an audit of your contribution to the parliamentary service have those four principles running through it like a stick of Millport rock? And for staff who have joined in the 20 years since the beginning, I urge you to read the report and bring those aspirations to work with you every day. This isn't just for staff though, I think there is a positivity, enthusiasm and joy in that report that deserves wider recognition, whether that is reminding yourself of it or discovering it for the first time.

Against the odds, we were ready for the election and the first days of the new Parliament. Let's fast-forward to 1 July 1999, the day when powers were formally transferred to Holyrood and the day when the official opening took place. My great friend Fiona Shaw, from the Official Report, and I were inexplicably given the roles of Royal Party Ushers – our job was to make sure that the Queen, the Duke of Edinburgh and the Duke of Rothesay were in the right place at the right time. After a few sleepless nights and many increasingly hysterical worst-case scenario chats between Fiona and me, the day dawned, and we found ourselves standing at the entrance to the Assembly Hall waiting for the carriage to arrive. Having given disapproving glances to the school kids in various states of untidiness (shirts untucked, ties only a few inches long, etc) who were the guard of honour, we did our duty and the ceremony went largely to plan.

Before we knew it, we had watched the Concorde and Red Arrows fly overhead and were walking back with the newly empowered MSPs back to HQ with cheering crowds, Saltires and great weather. I remember clearly thinking that the excitement and optimism that we had as staff wasn't just confined to the EH1 bubble – during the procession back, and the open-air concerts held that night, the sense that something good had happened, that positive change was in the air, was palpable. It energised us as staff – we were all pretty tired and experiencing the adrenalin downer that follows when a group of people had worked to a key common goal, getting the Parliament up and running, and that goal had been achieved.

It is impossible to expect those levels of enthusiasm, energy and wide-eyed wonder to be sustained in any situation and some of the things that followed the official opening brought reality crashing in. The tragic death of our first First Minister, the resignation of our second, the growing criticism about the Holyrood Building Project and hostile media commentary about the quality of debate did knock confidence in our mission and, speaking personally, in ourselves. Looking back, I don't think the very high expectations that had been set, or at least encouraged, were ever going to survive contact with reality.

There were times when it was a struggle to keep your eyes on the big picture and to acknowledge that the ambitions, we had for the Parliament were going to be tempered by events. I remember feeling very proprietorial about it all, getting frustrated with press criticism and feeling personally wounded if an MSP would make a justifiable criticism of how the Parliament was run. This was the down-side to the elation of the early days, and it took some time to appreciate what the wiser heads were telling me – it was an inevitable consequence of working in a political environment. So, my reflection for colleagues who work in legislatures is that you must reconcile yourself to the fact that when you work hard to provide the framework and environment for rigorous democratic and public debate, the outcome is often uncomfortable and irritating!

I am interested in the way staff feel about their organisation and the impact that external factors can have. Getting things done is important of course, but in institutions that are predominantly about people and shifting stakeholder views, the *way* those things are done should have equal priority. This is why I am banging on about how important it is to understand how staff are feeling and the effect that can have on getting things done.

I don't want to dwell too long on the Holyrood Building Project, and the injustice I feel still about how the people involved were treated by press and colleagues alike. But the opening of the new building in 2004 provides some interesting insights. The issues affecting the creation of the Parliament's new home have been covered in-depth over the years. What has not received much attention though is the impact of that firestorm on the wider objectives we were trying to achieve. It felt to me that no matter how well we were supporting scrutiny, whether through hard-hitting committee reports or Chamber business, we were valued purely based on our construction skills. A lot of political and management time was focused on this issue and although that was right, I felt that it skewed the value we were bringing to Scotland.

As I say, I raise this not as criticism but as a reminder that whatever is using up all the oxygen at any one time, it is critical to remember those staff who are valiantly trying to do the day job. They are not involved in the make or break meetings; they are not on the inside track of what is going to be in the papers and the 'fear of missing out' can affect those delivering the core business. The leadership team need to remember that and, next time it happens, remember to keep those people enthused and encouraged. This is something I will need to remember as the Palace of Westminster Restoration and Renewal Project gathers pace.

In a spectacular game of playing chicken with fate, Sir George Reid announced the opening ceremony of the new building in October 2004 at a time when, to put it mildly, there were some concerns about whether the building would be ready. History shows that he won that game of chicken and the Queen duly arrived on 9 October and declared it open. I was working in the Presiding Officer's Office then and it is fair to say that this was a stressful time. But there were also clear resonances with the heady days of 1999 – there was an explicitly defined goal, an immovable deadline, and I felt that the first day's spirit had returned. The Riding of Parliament down the Royal Mile brought back the cheering crowds and Saltires, the media narrative moved on to the architecture and the spectacle of the event and our tails were up.

What are the lessons then? Instilling a sense of purpose, enthusiasm and energy into parliamentary staff is relatively easy when there are big, narrowly defined and reputationally interesting events to be achieved. How do you keep that going during business as usual? How do you rediscover the passion and drive you had for the organisation when you first joined after well-publicised shocks or knocks hit you? These are questions not just for the Parliament's leadership, administrative and political, to consider for the next 20 years but also for those who work there. There is a responsibility on everyone for their workplace morale and for my former colleagues at Holyrood a re-read of the CSG report is not a bad place to start.


## Part 2: Westminster

In worse weather than I had ever experienced in my ten years in Edinburgh, I struggled into London on 3 January 2010 to start my secondment to the House of Commons. I started my career in the Commons working on the Savings Programme that had been put in place in response to the public expenditure environment at that time. So far, I have worked in the Speaker's Office, Communications and latterly leading the development of the Independent Complaints and Grievance Scheme, but I want to focus on my perceptions and experiences of the public engagement approach at the Commons.

Heading to Westminster I reflected on the early days of the Scottish Parliament. The CSG report was clear that it wanted Holyrood to embody a different style to that of Westminster. Where Westminster was perceived as patrician and remote, housed as it is in an imposing palace, Holyrood was meant to be different. Those of us working on setting up the procedures and systems took that cue, and it fair to say that we were guided by an informal 'anything but Westminster' approach.

I think it is also fair to say that there wasn't an awful lot of desire to import these new-fangled ideas down the A1 to Westminster. In the early days there were some tensions between MPs and MSPs about their respective roles, particularly in constituency work. There were unflattering, and unattributed, comments in the media about the quality of debates and emerging policy divergence – such as in free social care and tuition fees. Early suggestions for renaming the Scottish Executive fell on stony ground and Jack McConnell's work in Malawi also raised eyebrows.

It might be easy to draw the conclusion then that what we had was a stand-off between the old and the new, the sovereign and the devolved, the closed and the open. In my view that would be too simplistic an analysis. Yes, there were tensions politically and, with apologies to my current colleagues, indifference from Westminster staff to our overtures to engage and share. But the thaw came quickly. For example, it may be difficult to imagine now but the original procedures did not allow for First Minister's Questions (FMQs). It was felt that Prime Minister's Questions (PMQs) and the behaviour it triggered at Westminster was not the sort of thing for Holyrood.

Instead, there was a period called 'Open Questions' in which the First Minister could answer questions or could nominate another minister to do so. That proved unpopular with not only members and the media but also the First Minister and after just a few months FMQs were instituted. The thaw was not just one way though; Westminster soon became keen to work with Holyrood, particularly in the public engagement sphere that I will come on to shortly.

Some personal impressions first. Having come to Westminster from a relatively new organisation, with limited history and precedents, some of the differences were stark. On the surface the scale, architecture, procedure and culture were very different. Once I got to know the place, and the staff, there was more in common than you might have thought as you wandered through the always impressive Westminster Hall and the gothic brilliance of Augustus Pugin.

The passion and pride staff felt working for a legislature was not restricted to the relative newbies in Edinburgh and the commitment to ensuring democracy ran smoothly was just as keenly felt in London. Staff were also subject to similar shocks that impacted on how they felt about themselves and the institution they were working for. And, like Holyrood, there was a family feel amongst colleagues. It is fair to say that the House of Commons Service has been shaken by allegations of poor behaviour, but I think there is real commitment to tackling the workplace culture.

Back to the public engagement theme. I arrived, in the aftermath of the expenses issues that had hit the headlines in 2009, to the general sense that there was a need for change to happen. The title given to the report of the Reform of the House of Commons Committee (informally known as the Wright Committee after its chair Tony Wright) *Rebuilding the House* says it all about a mood shift following the expenses scandal. A series of motions in February and March 2010 gave the House's approval to, amongst others, a series of changes to the way committee chairs were elected, the introduction of the Backbench Business Committee and motions on public engagement.

Having worked in Holyrood, the motions around public engagement were particularly interesting. It was at this time that I think the CSG principles of sharing the power and engaging with the public began to resonate more clearly with our colleagues in Westminster. Devolution more widely had changed the landscape of representation in the UK, with an increased emphasis on local issues being tackled by local politicians. This, as well as the difficulties around expenses, was the midwife of a new commitment to trialling debates on public petitions and engaging the public on the legislative process.

There was a bit of 'been there, done that' for colleagues at Holyrood, but the significance of this new focus on the public was very important at Westminster. Another indicator of the change in atmosphere came with the agreement of the House to allow the UK Youth Parliament to meet in the Chamber once a year. It was not a unanimous agreement and took a couple of attempts to pass as some emotions ran high given that previously, the green benches had been for MPs only.

Alongside the political discussions, there were a small number of staff who were taking this agenda forward too and pushing for changes. Led by the Librarian of the House of Commons at the time, John Pullinger, the House Service soon began an outreach service and increased education and public engagement activity. I think it is not particularly helpful to talk about who was winning, but Holyrood had a head start in this due to the CSG and what is mentioned above. But once Westminster got hold of this agenda it was able to throw considerable effort, imagination and resource at it.

Over the past ten years, the outreach and engagement agenda has progressed significantly – from year-long, multimedia campaigns such as the 750-year commemorations of the Montfort Parliament (1265) and 800-year commemorations of the sealing of the Magna Carta (1215) in 2015 to the excellent commemoration of a hundred years since the first women were given the vote in 2018. As well as these large campaigns, UK Parliament Week 2018 reached 989,400 people in one week through the 8,108 face-to-face events and activities that took place in all 650 constituencies with an average of 12 activities per constituency.

We have also seen some excellent work take place with select committees. The Select Committee Engagement Team has made great strides in opening up committee work through facilitating consultation with the public before committee inquiries and on draft recommendations once the inquiry is complete; innovative use of film and voice recordings and, importantly, connecting the audiences that our Education and Engagement services already engage with to Select Committee inquiries. The vibrancy and innovation of the committee's work, plus impactful and challenging videos on the role of key legislation on people's day-to-day lives, such as the Race Relations Act, is a small taster of the work that Westminster is doing to engage the public.

Additionally, the opening of a dedicated Education Centre at Westminster has allowed us to welcome far more students to Parliament than previously and provide them with crucial knowledge of parliamentary democracy and the value of debate. This is augmented with the Teachers' Institute, a unique three-day intensive development programme for teachers which includes a Q&A with members of both Houses, activities to help develop classroom resources and in-depth knowledge of parliament and democracy.

## Conclusion

From a distance, I clearly am not as aware of the work that has been going on in engagement activity over the past ten years at Holyrood, but I think that if there were a 'race' then Westminster has pulled ahead. In my view, Westminster has become more innovative, less risk-averse and more evidence-based in its engagement work over the past ten years. I hesitate to compare in this way as there are material differences in size, resource availability, and so on, between the two institutions but looking to the next 20 years at Holyrood I wonder whether the political and administrative focus needs to be brought back to the engagement agenda?

Why is this important? The level of political discussion and debate in early 2019 is fraught to put it mildly. The role of technology and social media in disseminating inaccurate and hyperbolic views and news must surely motivate us who really care for, and work in, parliaments to redouble our efforts to try and cut through the noise. Democracy is precious and those of us who have been privileged to work for the institutions in facilitating democracy care deeply about it. We are uniquely placed to drive new ideas and encourage and empower our staff to find ways to find a way to cut through the cynicism.

As I said at the start, I think that how staff *feel* is an underestimated impact on the success of our organisations. Especially now, whilst we walk to work through the maelstroms of political crises and uncertainty, we are not immune to that. So, I say to our leaders, the key to the success of the next 20 years of the Scottish Parliament rests in encouraging and nurturing that innate pride and passion with which we walked up the Mound in 1999 and reminding us of the creativity we brought to making a brand-new democratic venture take hold.

CHAPTER 4

# The MSP's Role

## Alan Convery and David Parker

LIKE ALL ELECTED representatives, Members of the Scottish Parliament (MSPs) perform several roles. Sometimes these roles are complementary; at other times, MSPs may be pulled in different directions by the demands of party loyalty, constituency duties and policy interests. On any one day, MSPs might find themselves doing advocacy work for a constituent in the morning, attending a committee hearing with a government minister giving evidence before lunch and then providing their view on a piece of legislation in the afternoon. A reception for a charity or further meetings in the constituency may follow in the evening.

MSPs must switch between different ways of being a representative. We suggest there are broadly three 'modes' of being an MSP (with some areas of work requiring MSPs to draw on all three simultaneously): representative, legislator and scrutiniser. On election night, the focus is on the area that an MSP is elected to represent. However, once in the Parliament, MSPs' thoughts have to also turn to holding the government to account and participating in the law-making process. They may carry out these functions on their own, through their party, or as part of a parliamentary committee.

As the Scottish Parliament gains more powers, it is likely that the policy environment will grow more complex (particularly in terms of fiscal policy). It also means the Chamber will grow busier, which has implications for the ability of parliamentarians to maintain a liveable work-life balance.

## Representative

MSPs are elected to represent a constituency or a region in the Scottish Parliament. For many MSPs, representing that constituency or region is their first priority. The ways in which MSPs chose to represent their constituents is varied and to some degree is the choice of the MSP. How to represent that constituency or region, however, is not quite that straightforward.

First, representation depends upon the electoral incentives MSPs face and those electoral incentives are different for a constituency versus a regional member. Constituency members are elected in a winner-takes-all plurality election. Their names are listed on the ballot papers, and they serve a particular geographic area alone. Regional members, conversely, are not directly elected and represent one of the eight regional areas of Scotland with six other members. Voters select regional members by casting a second ballot where they vote for a party. Seats are then allocated by a formula taking into account the number of constituencies seats each party wins in the region and the percentage of the vote cast on the second ballot. Regional members are then selected, in order, from a list submitted by each party to fill the seats won.

Although constituency and regional members are afforded the same rights and responsibilities, the ways in which MSPs are selected electorally creates the possibility of two different types of representatives focused on different types of representational activities to serve their constituents. Constituency members, serving a smaller geographic area alone and running for election with their names on the ballot, are incentivised to create a closer personal connection to the communities and people they represent. One obvious way to do this is to focus on constituency service. Constituency service representatives solve problems for constituents. They encourage constituents to bring problems to them, travel to the local area extensively and are more likely to hold constituency surgeries. They are visible in the local papers, and are champions of local businesses, industries and causes. Constituency MSPs who prefer the constituency service role do it not only because they care deeply about the people they represent, but also because it establishes a deep connection that constituents can easily reward come election time. In short, the constituency service role allows MSPs to develop a personal reputation with constituents beyond the record of their party, which can make them more electorally secure by protecting them against partisan tides should they turn against the MSPs' party in the future.

List MSPs, alternatively, are less likely to adopt a constituency service persona as a representative. This is not because they do not care about the problems their constituents might face navigating government bureaucracy or their views on policy matters, but because such work does not easily yield electoral benefits in quite the same way it does for constituency members. First, they represent a much larger geographic area that they share with six other members plus the constituency members in each region. The size of the region, plus competition with other members, simply makes it harder to do casework. However, the Code of Conduct for MSPs requires that regional MSPs work in more than two constituencies in their region.

Second, although both list and constituency MSPs are listed on the ballot because party electorates have chosen them, list MSP are much more beholden to the party and its success than constituency members. List members are ranked by party members, with a low ranking as tantamount to defeat as deselection altogether. At the same time, a regional MSP could more readily lose their seat through no fault of their own if the electorate turns against their party. As a result, regional MSPs are more likely to be active on the floor of the Scottish Parliament, making motions supportive of the party and engaging in the policy-making process to advance the party's legislative agenda. In this manner, the different electoral incentives create the possibility of two broadly different representational styles in the Scottish Parliament. In general, constituency MSPs do more constituency service work, while regional MSPs concern themselves more with policy and party branding activities. However, there is also evidence that regional members who aspire to represent a constituency engage in 'shadowing' behaviour, attempting to build up a profile in a particular constituency so that it is easier to win at election time. Both list and constituency MSPs, regardless of the representational role they choose, find themselves constantly involved in communicating their Holyrood work to the folks back home via press releases, emails and newsletters detailing their daily activities. In so doing, all MSPs strive to show their constituents that they are 'one of them' and are looking out for their interests in Parliament.

## Legislator

Beyond representation, a key function of any legislature is to make laws. The Scottish Parliament has passed 281 bills since 1999. MSPs play the central role in this process. In committee and in the main Chamber, MSPs have to consider draft laws not only as they affect their constituents but also how they address wider public policy issues. In this mode, MSPs are encouraged with the help of clerks and specialist researchers to become temporary policy experts. Unlike at Westminster, there is no distinction between legislative and select committees in the Scottish Parliament. Therefore, MSPs on the Education and Skills Committee, for instance, are expected to build up knowledge of a policy area both through writing reports and dealing with legislation (although in practice high turnover of members has made this aim difficult to achieve).

In the main Chamber, MSPs sit in their party groups. In this context, MSPs are encouraged to think of themselves as tribally linked to their colleagues, especially at set-piece events such as First Minister's Questions. Their role here is a party political one. Many MSPs will want to ask supportive questions of ministers if their party is in power and generally cheer and encourage whoever is speaking for their party on a particular issue. This mode of behaviour is analogous to displaying loyalty to your favourite sports team. In committees, however, the idea is that MSPs leave their party affiliation at the door and work much more cohesively to examine and improve legislation. In practice, it has often been difficult for MSPs to leave the mood of the Chamber behind. Committees reflect the party balance from the Chamber and government MSPs are naturally inclined to support their party's legislation. Moreover, in a system where committees are such a central part of the legislative process, it is natural that the governing party takes a keen interest in what goes on there. The legislative role of MSPs, therefore, is therefore inevitably tinged with party political considerations.

There is scope for MSPs to work together in committees to achieve legislative change. Scottish Parliament committees can produce their own draft laws and pilot them through the entire legislative process without requiring government initiative. This mode of working together across party lines has had some notable successes (for example, the Commissioner for Children and Young People (Scotland) Bill). However, only seven committee bills have been successfully passed since 1999. Two committee bills were passed during the period of minority government (2007–11), but there have been none since. It seems therefore that MSPs tend to see their legislative role as checkers and changers, rather than as policy initiators.

In addition, MSPs can attempt to steer their own legislation through Parliament by proposing a members' bill. There have been 54 members' bills introduced since 1999. MSPs may also use members' bills to highlight particular issues that they want the government to consider or to demonstrate to constituents that they are working hard on a particular issue with local importance. Clerks assist MSPs in drafting and introducing these bills. A members' bill proposal can be introduced as legislation if it receives the support of 18 MSPs and at least half of the Chamber's parties. Twenty members' bills (37 per cent of those introduced) have been enacted into law since the Scottish Parliament was established, but that is less than 10 per cent of the total legislation enacted.

MSPs involve themselves in the legislative process by offering amendments to bills, participating in legislative debates and drafting legislation both in committee and as standalone members' bills. However, it is clear the Government dominates the legislative process both in the number of bills introduced and the amount of time spent on government initiative legislation. Between 2004 and 2017, 47 per cent of chamber time, on average, has been devoted to government legislation, debate and motions. More notably, the percentage of time devoted to government legislation (as opposed to committee or members' bills) has increased substantially. In the 2004–05 session, 77 per cent of legislative time was devoted to government bills. This increased to 96 per cent in the 2016–17 session.

This pattern does not mean that MSPs are irrelevant; indeed, the government constructs legislation with the policy preferences of its party members in mind. But the dominance of the Government in the production of legislation and the expectation that MSPs rarely break with their party on votes on legislation suggests that the Scottish Parliament is perhaps more similar to Westminster than MSPs would care to admit. It also suggests that even newly formed legislative institutions are similarly prone to encroaching on executive authority and that extra efforts are necessary to prevent legislative functions from increasing executive encroachment.


## Scrutiniser

The Scottish Parliament's committees also have another central function: to scrutinise or oversee the work of the Scottish Government and its ministers. MSPs hear evidence, question witnesses and produce reports with the assistance of the clerks. Here, MSPs not only ask questions of a political nature (why was this not in the governing party's manifesto or why has my constituent still not had her operation despite this policy change?). They are also expected to play the role of 'policy wonk' in order to ask detailed questions about the cost, administration and effectiveness of the Government's work (what evidence do you have that this policy is working or why has there been such a high turnover of staff at this government agency?). Switching into this scrutiniser mode can be difficult. MSPs may have to move swiftly from one complicated policy area to another (eg student loan repayments to primary school testing) and have to find the time (among their other roles) to read and digest a large volume of evidence. It is especially challenging when MSPs serve on more than one committee or have to combine their committee work with duties in the Chamber as their party's principal spokesperson on a particular issue. The incentives to behave like a parliamentarian rather than a permanent party campaigner are principled rather than electoral. MSPs might safely assume that not many constituents tune in to watch committee hearings online.

When producing reports about what they have examined, the optimum outcome is that they are unanimous – although party loyalties sometimes make this difficult to achieve. A committee report agreed by all members of the committee across all parties (government and opposition) is likely to have more impact than one containing sections to which some MSPs object. Again, the MSPs' role here might involve putting party political considerations to one side. The role of the convener in building trust and managing tensions here is central to how well MSPs work together on committees. However, even in contentious policy areas, it has been possible to produce unanimous reports with recommendations. For instance, the Finance and Constitution Committee managed in 2018 to produce a unanimous report on the Brexit negotiations between the UK and Scottish Governments, despite the very different positions held by SNP and Scottish Conservative members in particular.

The other important way in which MSPs scrutinise is by asking questions of government ministers, either orally or in writing. The Scottish Parliament established the process of requiring ministers to submit to parliamentary enquiries regularly and publicly from its earliest proceedings, with the First Minister appearing each Thursday at noon. Although FMQS receives the most attention, MSPs also ask questions of ministers and the Scottish Parliamentary Corporate Body during Topical, Portfolio and General Question Times. Given the limited time for oral questions, not all questions lodged are asked and the process by which questions are selected varies. For example, the Presiding Officer has discretion in selecting questions for FMQs and Topical Questions, while MSPs interested in asking a General or Portfolio question submit their names (but not the questions) to a random electronic draw. Written questions, alternatively, can be submitted at any time and ministers are expected to produce an answer within ten days.

The effectiveness of parliamentary questions, written and oral, as a tool for scrutinising government action is debatable. While there is no research on public perceptions of Question Time at the Scottish Parliament, the British public has expressed some frustration with the perceived point scoring at Prime Minister's Questions designed more to attract media attention than engage in substantive oversight of the government. One recent examination of FMQs and written questions in the Scottish Parliament by David Parker, Jessie Munson and Caitlyn Richter shows that MSPs from the governing party are less likely to lodge written questions while asking more helpful questions of the government during FMQs than critical or neutral questions. And while the amount of time devoted to FMQs has increased, with the Presiding Officer adding an additional 15 minutes each week for a total of 45 minutes, the Scottish Parliament devotes less time to Question Time than the Parliament at Westminster on average: 14 versus 24 per cent over the period from 2004 through 2017.

## Conclusion

MSPs must be versatile. In their own office or constituency, they may be at the top of the tree and able to dictate events. In the Chamber or committee, they may find themselves in a minority, working to make arguments and build consensus. Good MSPs switch modes easily from local champion to policy wonk or cheerleader. Clerks may want MSPs to spend more time on briefing documents than casework, but clerks will still have a job after the next election, regardless of the result; MSPs might not.

As the Scottish Parliament looks forward to its next 20 years, we conclude by outlining three challenges MSPs face: the devolution of additional responsibilities from Westminster, the diversity of experiences among MSPs necessary to contribute to a representative and vibrant Parliament and the informal division of responsibilities between regional and constituency MSPs.

One result of the 2014 independence referendum is the increased power devolved to the Scottish Parliament, including more control over fiscal and welfare policy. These powers, however, require MSPs to shoulder more responsibility as representatives, legislators and scrutinisers, which has the potential to upend the careful work-life balance the Scottish Parliament has established since its inception. The Chamber spends far less time in session compared to Westminster. Between 2004 and 2017, MPs sat for nearly 1,100 hours. MSPs at Holyrood, conversely, sat on average for 402 hours over the same period – or 63 per cent less. However, the number of hours MSPs spent in session has been on the rise, with time in session increasing by 14 per cent since 2004. It is likely to increase additionally with more responsibilities handed over to Holyrood in the recent Scotland Act. And the additional time in chamber is only one aspect of an MSPs' workload that may increase: constituents will have more concerns to voice and more problems to solve as the Scottish Parliament is responsible for more policy production and the spending of more money. Will MSPs simply have to work more, and if so, what consequence does that have for their personal lives and the ability to recruit quality candidates to serve in the Chamber? It may be time, perhaps, to consider increasing the size of the Chamber to respond to these new demands rather than expect existing MSPs to shoulder the burdens of this increased workload alone.

Consequently, how the Scottish Parliament addresses its increased workload has important implications for another form of representation: descriptive. Descriptive representation is the notion that representation is not simply programmatic but requires parliamentarians to reflect constituents physically in terms of their ethnicity and gender. As it stands currently, women and ethnic minorities are under-represented in the Scottish Parliament compared to Scotland's population. Only 40 per cent of MSPs are women in the current parliamentary session and less than 2 per cent come from an ethnic minority background. Although increasing the number of women and ethnic minorities serving is largely the responsibility of the parties selecting candidates to stand in constituencies and on the regional lists, the Scottish Parliament must remain cognizant and vigilant against establishing processes and procedures discouraging women and ethnic minorities from considering a career in the Chamber. These considerations may include refraining from Westminster's late- or all-night sessions, establishing an official maternity policy for MSPs, or, most radically, perhaps formally instituting ethnic and gender quotas for the Chamber.

Another point bears consideration: Scotland is getting older, which suggests a host of implications financially for the Scottish state that include how to pay for generous pension and healthcare provisions with fewer workers to contribute. With increased taxation powers especially, the Scottish Parliament must resolve this difficult cross-generational challenge. Although the Chamber roughly approximates the median age of Scotland so that an aging population can rest easy knowing that their interests will be protected, the fundamental challenge facing representative democracy is that cost burdens rest most heavily on future generations that do not yet have the franchise. Extending the right of 16- and 17-year-olds to vote in Scottish Parliamentary elections is one key step not only because of this inter-generation resource imbalance but also to attempt to spur increased interest in the Scottish Government and its affairs at an earlier age. This change may also help to resolve the other issue: encouraging younger candidates to run for office and increase the prospect that the concerns of the younger generation are properly aired and represented in the Chamber.

Finally, over the past 20 years, a clear division of labour between MSPs appears to have developed, with constituency MSPs engaged in more constituency service work than regional members – that is, up to a certain point. Clearly, for those seeking to establish a career in the Scottish Parliament, serving as a constituency MSP has the potential for more job security over the long-term because constituency members can develop a personal electoral brand that voters can more easily recall come election time. Regional members, however, are in a more precarious situation electorally because they are not listed on the ballot and find themselves competing with the other six MSPs serving in the same region. As a result, regional MSPs often carve up the region amongst themselves and focus their policy and casework efforts primarily in one particular constituency they intend to contest come the next election (and, perhaps, they contested in the previous election). Therefore, certain constituencies within a region, likely the more marginal ones, may find themselves with a representational surplus whilst others may have a relative representational deficit. That is to say that the desire for regional MSPs to enjoy the greater electoral security of a constituency seat may mean, perversely, that certain constituencies and geographic areas may receive less attention and fewer resources than others simply because these places are less attractive for multiple regional MSPs to contest in future elections. At the very least, the Scottish Parliament should remain aware of the potential drawbacks of a Chamber populated by MSPs serving in multi-member regions alongside those representing single constituencies.

As Nelson Polsby wrote about the US Congress 50 years ago,

> it is generally agreed that for a political system to be in some sense free and democratic, means must be found for institutionalising representativeness with all the diversity that this implies, and for legitimising yet at the same time containing political opposition within the system.

The Scottish Parliament has been 'institutionalising representativeness' over the past 20 years, but in so doing, it is perhaps time to pause and consider whether the manner in which the Scottish Parliament has institutionalised, particularly in terms of member roles, best serves the Scottish people moving forward. Is the division of responsibilities that has informally developed between regional and constituency members problematic for representation and work within the Chamber? Should Scotland consider, instead, a bicameral legislature with regional members populating one Chamber and constituency members the other? With the increased powers obtained post-referendum and the additional responsibilities this entails; would it make sense to develop a system of select committees working on a cross-party basis to scrutinise and oversee government operations more aggressively? The Scottish Parliament expresses that it values stewardship, inclusiveness, excellence and respect. Whether the manner in which MSP roles have become routinised and established are consistent with those values is perhaps worthy of inspection and consideration not just on the Chamber's 20th anniversary, but routinely and regularly.

*Dear Scottish Parliament...*

I think all kids in Primary school should have a fund for artistic purposes. This could be a £500 learning fund to help towards creative skills such as music lessons, singing, photography, music technology, dancing, public speaking.

I believe that most kids out there will have untapped potential in a creative skill, so much talent is probably undiscovered which is a huge gigantic loss for everyone in Scotland.

Not only will these lessons help children express themselves it will help them with confidence and no doubt will improve their wellbeing.

The Parliament needs to fix this and quickly so every kid gets a chance to try these things and not just rich people who can afford it. Imagine growing up and not ever experiencing the more creative side of things.

All children deserve the chance to thrive. The fund could be used for anything: lessons, cultural trips or buying an instrument.

My hopes are that the Scottish Parliament continues to work with young people, inviting them in.

I feel very proud of our Scottish Parliament and one day would love to come for a visit. All kids should also get the opportunity to see their Scottish Parliament to experience the building, the people and see what it does each day. I would love to come for a visit some time.

I have done my schoolwork experience with the Scottish Government in Atlantic Quay in Glasgow, it was an amazing experience and I would like to use this opportunity to thank everyone for their help.

In the future I want to study psychology to help young people with their mental health.

Good luck to the Scottish Parliament and I hope you are also living your dreams.

*Claire Hossack, 15, South Lanarkshire*

CHAPTER 5

# Parliament and Business:

## An Unfulfilled Relationship?

MICHAEL CROW

AT THE HEART of the Scottish Parliament sits the mace, a gift from Her
Majesty the Queen which, in the words of the late Donald Dewar,

> is a symbol of the great democratic tradition from which we draw our
> inspiration and our strength.

This royal donation has commanded respect and defined the values of
the Parliament over the last two decades.

A lesser known gift is a gavel given to the Presiding Officer at the
beginning of the Parliament by a group of business people. Symbolising
the authority and power that the Speaker holds over MSPs in the Chamber, this gavel plays a much smaller but nevertheless intriguing part in
the history of Holyrood. Seen by some as a delightful offering, others
have questioned whether it was actually a business community in-joke.
Always wary of uncertainty, business was initially lukewarm in its support for devolution and some speculated that the gift of the gavel was a
symbol of the control business hoped to exert over the Parliament as it
established itself again in Scotland after a 300-year absence.

In-joke or not, the story captures the relationship between two pillars
of Scottish society; a relationship that, over the last 20 years, has perhaps never managed to be as close and productive as many might have
hoped. This was despite Donald Dewar in the early days trying to reas-
sure business about his commitment to the sector by appointing business
heavyweight Lord Gus Macdonald to look after the Scottish industry
brief in the Scottish Office and then, for his first Cabinet, creating a new
Enterprise, Transport and Lifelong Learning Department to send a signal to business that the Scottish Government was focused on economic
growth and the future, rather than the past.

Pollster Mark Diffley:

Chief among business concerns were that around a third thought it would lead to higher taxation and less clout internationally, and around a quarter thought it would create more bureaucracy. So, although negativity was not universal, it is important to recognise the significant unease there was in the period between the referendum of 1997 and the establishment of the new Parliament in 1999.

Perhaps understandably, a strong relationship between the Parliament and business never really flourished in the initial years of devolution. I say understandably for two reasons. Firstly, the economy was doing well so the Parliament didn't really need to focus on business and on the other side business didn't really need to engage with the Parliament. In 1997, Scotland's GDP increased by over 5 per cent, the fastest pace of growth since 1973, while real income per person had been rising by around 2.5 per cent per annum in the years leading up to devolution. Incomes were set to accelerate in the first few years after the Parliament was re-established.

Stephen Blackman, Principal Economist at RBS says this was an economically successful period for Scotland in a number of ways:

The period also coincided with a turning point in Scotland's business, social and economic landscape. In a significant reversal, after almost 50 years of slowdown and then outright decline, Scotland's population started to increase. In the years between devolution and 2007, Scotland's population rose by nearly 90,000, having fallen by just over 20,000 in the decade to 1997. And Scotland's on-shore economy expanded by more than a quarter (28 per cent) between 1998 and 2007, with the drivers firmly within Scotland's growing service economy.

The second reason the fledgling Parliament and business were slow to forge a close relationship was because newly elected MSPs were finding their feet and focusing on areas where they wielded power, (such as the spending departments of health and education), or had a political interest in (such as land reform, fox hunting, Section 28, the smoking ban and free school meals). If that didn't keep them busy then they had their pay to discuss, a building to complete and emergencies such as the

Noel Ruddle case to deal with. The Parliament also had no real incentive to generate economic growth or engage with business because it simply didn't need to. It received a generous block grant from Westminster and had few tax raising powers, so the incentive and the tools were not there. Holyrood instead focused on addressing the legislative backlog built up when Scottish legislation had been at the back of the Westminster queue.

Business was not top of the Parliament's agenda but that is not to say it wasn't considered important. Changes were introduced and progress was made, although, as the then Enterprise Minister Wendy Alexander says, the result of much of this work was to take years to emerge:

> There were vital steps in the name of social justice and economic progress, like the introduction of the National Minimum Wage at Westminster, but most of the measures to improve economic performance were to be altogether less eye catching and a slower burn. Many of the best institutional and legislative reforms have outlasted the administration that introduced them. And the instincts for cross-party consensus building, particularly around Scotland's positioning overseas has been a recurring feature over the intervening two decades, although under-recognised.

Scottish Development International was created to focus on international trade; modern apprenticeships were encouraged through the new deal task force; GlobalScot was set up to engage with the Scottish diaspora; enterprise education was promoted in schools and new university and industry links were championed. Wendy Alexander tried to generate some serious interest in the economy with her strategic programme Smart, Successful Scotland. For the first time Scotland's performance was benchmarked to the Organisation for Economic Co-operation and Development (OECD) in its own right – a change that still exists today. But this report also identified Scotland's relatively poor performance in OECD national productivity rankings, persistently low levels of business R&D, subdued new business birth rates and comparatively poor digital connections and her vision to create a fast learning, high earning, globally connected nation, where every Scot was ready for tomorrow's jobs, remained just that – a vision.

Over the years Parliament has made thousands of similar nods in the direction of business but few have managed to generate any substantial cross-party consensus and have as a result not managed to get beyond the vision stage. Wendy Alexander again:

> Two decades of opposition to Conservative rule had provided the glue for Scotland's pro-devolution forces, compelling even the SNP to support the case for a devolved parliament as a stepping stone to independence. However as soon as the Parliament was established, and the elections contested by political parties, it was inevitable that party politics would determine the character of both the new Scottish Government and the legislature. Consequently, the sustained national consensus many Conventioneers had dreamed of was never going to survive the advent of an elected Parliament.

The business sector itself was also partly to blame for a lack of any substantial engagement with Parliament during these early years. The traditional political champions of business, the Scottish Conservatives, were still finding their feet having been marginalised by their opposition to devolution, so business couldn't rely on its natural allies to speak out on its behalf. But the sector also failed to find a way of speaking with one voice, setting the agenda or influencing parliamentarians in a meaningful way. The opportunity was there but it was never really taken.

Once the SNP was elected in 2007, matters became even more complex for business as there were different governments north and south of the border and the colour of both parliaments was very different. Partisanship became even more acute in 2011 when the SNP won an overall majority in the Scottish Parliament and the constitution rapidly rose to the top of the political agenda. The latest contribution to a business and economic strategy for Scotland, Andrew Wilson's Sustainable Growth Commission, may be a thought-provoking piece of work but, given it was commissioned by First Minister Nicola Sturgeon as a route-map to independence, even the non-independence focused proposals are unlikely to gain cross-party support.

By the 2007 Scottish elections Holyrood had found its feet and was established as an important institution in Scotland. Gone were the teething troubles and in its place a new confidence emerged, and voters also felt confident enough to break away from Scottish Labour. The new SNP government, elected in May 2007, was determined to prove it was capable of governing and governing well, and this included building a solid relationship with business.

During 2007–11 the constitutional agenda within the Scottish Parliament was primarily driven by the Calman Commission on Scottish devolution which was established by a Scottish Labour Party motion passed on 6 December 2007, with the support of the Scottish Conservatives and Scottish Liberal Democrats. The SNP opposed the creation of the Commission. The focus of the SNP minority administration was not on the constitution but rather its priority was to establish itself as a competent and credible government.

There was much talk about the Arc of Prosperity, with First Minister Alex Salmond comparing Scotland to Ireland, Iceland and Norway and arguing that those countries had developed much more quickly than Scotland because they were independent and had been able to take action to develop their economies such as lowering business taxes. We saw the formation of the Council of Economic Advisers which brought together Nobel Prize winners, the private sector and academia to improve the competitiveness of the Scottish economy and tackle inequality. Business and parliament were engaged, and the Cabinet Secretary for Finance, Employment and Sustainable Growth John Swinney was central to laying the foundation of this good relationship:

> Over many years, a number of us in the SNP team built up good relationships with many in the business community. By the time we won in 2007, that quiet, patient dialogue gave us a good foundation to engage the business community and take an approach that involved them closely in a national effort to strengthen the economy. That effort was given an even sharper focus by the financial crisis which required us to take swift, bold and pragmatic steps to ensure economic recovery. The fact that we navigated our way through such turbulence, with a lower increase in unemployment than many expected and with an activist mentality to support businesses in difficulty, deepened the relationship between the SNP and business. These approaches, coupled to a very tight grip on the public finances, earned for the SNP a sturdy reputation for economic and fiscal management that we previously never commanded. That record of economic competence was one of the crucial factors in our emphatic electoral success in 2011.

A raft of business measures was guided through parliament by John Swinney, specifically designed to encourage growth and improve business confidence. Reform of Scottish Enterprise, a single skills body, rates relief for small businesses, parity with the rest of the UK on business rates and the abolition of tolls on the Forth and Tay Bridges to name but a few. Ambitious infrastructure projects such as the Forth Replacement Crossing and the Aberdeen Western Peripheral Route were pushed through. They were so business friendly that the Scottish Conservatives were able to put aside their substantial differences with the minority administration and support its budget, as summed up by the late David McLetchie speaking in the 2009 budget debate:

> I express my deep gratitude to the Labour and Liberal Democrat parties in the Parliament, whose sheer incompetence and ineptitude over the course of the budget negotiations enabled the Scottish Conservatives to win concessions totalling £234 million from the SNP Government, which all Labour and Liberal Democrat members will end up voting for. That is what I call a real achievement. Let us face it: the next best thing to a Tory Government is a Government that does what the Tories tell it to do and whose policies Opposition parties vote for in any case.

Senior business leaders were courted assiduously by the Salmond administration and especially by First Minister Alex Salmond himself, whose background as an RBS economist meant he was comfortable in the company of business leaders. As a minority administration it was necessary for the new SNP Government to build these relationships with as many organisations and people as possible. Geoff Aberdein, Chief of Staff for Alex Salmond, was instrumental in building the business relationships:

> The First Minister was very keen to focus on the business community and as a result his office organised a lot of calls, meetings and visits. Every Friday we spent time phoning around business people in Scotland listening to what they had to say and explaining what we were doing. We built a very strong relationship with key players in Scotland and ensured our Programme for Government was well informed and focused on business needs. Any government worth its salt would do the same thing.

Any Parliament worth its salt would also have been doing the same thing but while the Scottish Government was leading the way, the main focus of the Parliament was still, as it had been in its early years, on issues such as health, social justice and education. Parliamentary committees and cross-party groups were still not carrying out major inquiries into economic growth and neither were they holding the Scottish Government to account on what was working for business and what wasn't. Business was still not being engaged at a parliamentary level and attempts by companies to hold sessions on issues such as productivity, infrastructure or the economy were very poorly attended.

The focus of the Parliament was elsewhere but a good business relationship was seen as essential by the minority administration, not only to enhance the SNP's credibility in government but to also prove a point – independence was not something to fear. However, the financial crash changed all that.

The first ten years of the Parliament was, in economic terms, relatively stable giving both business and Parliament the time to find their feet, grow and mature in the new political construct. The next ten years have been almost the exact opposite. In fact, according to the Fraser of Allander Institute, Scotland's GDP per head grew 2 per cent per annum between 2000 and 2008 and 2 per cent in total between 2008 and 2016

The financial crisis followed by the constitutional challenges of the independence referendum, and then Brexit, has seen a long period of uncertainty and change. To make it worse the two banks at the heart of the financial crisis, RBS and HBOS, had long, and some would argue distinguished, histories in Scotland. Their downfall was keenly felt not just in the pockets, but in the hearts, of many Scots. Many businesses and households were also supported by the two banks and their fall from grace could have been disastrous had it not been for two Scots in power at Westminster, Chancellor Alistair Darling and Prime Minister Gordon Brown, who bailed out the banks to the tune of £500 billion and stabilised the UK economy.

The solutions to the financial crisis were entirely constructed at Westminster with the Scottish Parliament playing a much lesser role because it didn't have the levers to contribute meaningfully. However, Holyrood once again showed its limited interest in business by largely leaving the inquiries into what went wrong to Westminster. At the time of the crisis RBS was the biggest bank in the world and HBOS was the sixth largest bank in Europe. Both banks were based in Scotland but MSPs largely left it to MPs to investigate the crash and the consequences of the financial crisis.

In the end, Scotland suffered slightly less from the fallout of the crisis in 2008–09 compared to the rest of the UK. Economic activity in Scotland fell by 4 per cent between the middle of 2008 and the end of 2009 while in the UK it fell by more than 6 per cent. Catherine MacLeod was a special adviser in the Treasury during the crisis:

> Alistair and Gordon frantically and successfully mobilised to stop economic collapse. They weren't interested in playing party politics, and perhaps in retrospect they missed a trick. Both of them were highly aware of the devastating effect the banks' failures had on the lives of many people in Scotland, not just in business but in the personal lives of many of their constituents and they worked day and night with their colleagues in the Treasury.

By the time the 2011 Scottish Parliament elections were held the SNP reaped the rewards of a number of aligning stars and won an overall majority in Holyrood. The SNP minority administration had proved itself to many to be fit for government and in touch with, and sympathetic to, numerous interest groups in Scotland, including business. Westminster, despite averting what could have been an economic meltdown, was blamed by the public for not regulating the banks properly or holding them to account for the crash. MPs were at the same time engulfed by the expenses scandal. The Scottish Tories, still despised in some sections of Scottish society, were in office after the 2010 UK election exacerbating the lack of consensus between the parliaments and governments. Finally, the Liberal Democrats were propping up the Tories at Westminster and as a result suffered electorally in Scotland. It was a SNP triumph many never thought possible, but it was also a result that was to lead to a significant change in the relationship between the Parliament and business.

Quite simply the election result in 2011, which saw the SNP gain an overall majority in the Scottish Parliament, meant that an independence referendum was inevitable. The result of that referendum was close enough for the Scottish Parliament to secure more powers – especially in the area of tax raising powers. In fact, the Scottish Government block grant will fall from more than 80 per cent of Scotland's revenue mix in 2015 to around 50 per cent in 2019 as even more tax powers are devolved. As a result, the relationship between the Parliament and business is now more important than ever. Gone are the days when business and economic growth were not a priority. Spending departments must now rely on the tax raising effectiveness of the Scottish Government. The relationship muscle that should bind Parliament and business together, and which has probably not always been exercised properly in the past, can no longer be allowed to go slack.

Constitutional change, whether in the EU or the UK, including the devolution of substantial further fiscal and borrowing powers, has always worried many in the business community. The fact that the relationship between business and Parliament has never been as strong as it could have been just exacerbates this problem. However, uncertainty is almost becoming the new norm. In hindsight, devolution in 1999 was a cake-walk compared to where we are now 20 years later and where we could be in the next decade as a result of innovation and technology. The so-called Fourth Industrial Revolution could be a huge opportunity for Scotland, or it could be a major threat. Businessman Sir Tom Hunter is worried:

> If you grasp that the pace of change is the fastest it's ever been but the slowest it will ever be, you'd understand why we need business, education and politicians – parliamentarian and councillors – to coalesce around building for the future, not the past.
>
> We need to prepare Scotland's future, our young people, for jobs that don't even exist today – by reinventing education. Public service delivery has to change and so too business preparedness for a digital and AI age that is simply not going away.
>
> It's easy to focus on the past and the here and now, we need the vision to deliver now for future generations. For that we need agility, speed and focus from all concerned.
>
> If we are to succeed in building the economy, it is the entrepreneurs and businesses that generate the tax, not the politicians. It is high time we worked far more together in building Scotland's future, we are a small nation and can and should lead the world in this the Fourth Industrial Revolution.

Brexit, the issue of independence and a new tax regime could be nothing compared to this revolution. A report by the think tank Centre for Cities suggests that in Scotland's four largest cities alone 20 per cent of jobs could be affected. However, Elena Magrini, an analyst at the think tank, says the rise of automation and AI could actually see more jobs being created but unless strategic action is taken by governments and parliaments, in collaboration with business, there is also the risk that the opportunity may be missed.

> In recent years, interpersonal and analytical skills such as customer awareness, creative thinking and problem solving have become ever more important in the labour market, but places more vulnerable to automation are also the places that tend to see poorer education outcomes. Urgent and concerted action is needed to address these issues and to develop an education system able to provide current and future workers with the skills they need to prosper. Only in this way we will be able to turn the threat of automation into an opportunity.

What makes the current changes different to previous 'industrial' revolutions is that AI could reach right across the jobs' spectrum – not just jobs that we would regard as mundane and repetitive. As a result, and the speed at which it might happen, it has the potential to leave many people behind. Pollster Mark Diffley believes this threat is one of the major challenges facing parliamentarians and business today:

> As businesses strive to capitalise on the opportunities offered by AI and the Fourth Industrial Revolution, many people are anxious, particularly for what it may mean for their jobs. Recent research shows that more than half of people in Britain think that more jobs will be lost than gained as a result of automation in the next 15 years and that around a quarter are concerned about losing their own jobs. Parliamentarians are likely to share the concern of voters and highlight the potential social risks of AI.

Wendy Alexander's vision to create a fast learning, high earning, globally connected nation, where every Scot is ready for tomorrow's jobs, is still just a vision almost 20 years later. Parliament and business have never managed to find a way of working well enough together to find solutions to the issues of the day, evaluate what policies work and what don't and implement a long-term business strategy for Scotland. This has been a missed opportunity (not just in Scotland) and, with the advent of the Fourth Industrial Revolution, righting those wrongs is now more important than ever.

We cannot continue to focus on 'better yesterdays', repeating the same old political arguments in the same old areas. Business people and politicians need to find a new way of building a consensus to face the future – be that opportunities or threats. We need a long-term vision and plan rather than something tied to the electoral cycle. We need to accept uncertainty but get better at risk management. We need to get beyond transient initiatives and false starts to a shared agenda that is cross-party, long-term and delivers a joined up economic strategy. The failure by both business and Parliament to develop a strong relationship over the last 20 years must also be addressed.

There are more than a hundred cross-party groups in the Scottish Parliament but less than 5 per cent have anything to do with business. None are focusing on the Fourth Industrial Revolution. Business people and parliamentarians need to work out how they can build a relationship going forward. Businesses need to be prepared to give up the time and open their doors to MSPs to spend time with them and see what goes on. Parliamentarians need to be open to listening to business and not see big business, in particular, as bad. There are some world leaders from business working in Scotland, including in tech, and parliament needs to hear what they have to say – but without prejudice. Too often when a business makes a difficult decision based on sound reasoning MSPs will be quick to condemn it because it gathers votes, rather than looking at the business rational behind the decision and trying to understand the long-term strategic plan. On the other side business sometimes makes a decision without explaining to MSPs properly why it has been made. Trust between the two bodies is regularly lost and without proper engagement then this will only get worse. More business people standing as MSPs would go a long way to helping to solve this problem.

Ever the optimist I believe the gavel that was gifted to the fledgling Scottish Parliament by business was in good faith. It was a sign of business willing to work with politicians for the good of the country. That has not always been the case over the years for a variety of reasons, but more and more it is becoming a necessity. To mitigate the risks and seize the opportunities of issues such as constitutional change, the Fourth Industrial Revolution or climate change it is imperative that parliament and business collaborate. If that doesn't happen then we will miss the opportunities and exacerbate the threats.

*Dear Scottish Parliament...*

My wish is to see the Scottish Parliament growing, developing and building greater relationships over the next 20 years.

There are already brilliant initiatives in place encouraging the young into politics however I am sure there is much more we can do.

We have the Youth Parliament but how does a young person get to hear about this? How are they encouraged to get involved? I think there could be much more done to strengthen the communication between the Scottish Parliament and schools. I want to see all schools and pupils having access to a single database that has every single opportunity to learn and develop available to students throughout the UK so every young person can apply and be considered for opportunities to grow, whether that be initiatives, funded trips and educational opportunities.

I want to see positive discrimination, I think Scotland is leading the way in encouraging minority groups into Parliament, but I want this to continue to develop.

I am so thrilled to be part of the YWCA this year and want to encourage young girls who don't know these opportunities are available to put themselves forward as it raises aspirations and Parliament benefits from a broad range of ideas.

I would like to see the young in our Parliament being given opportunities to go to Europe, London and worldwide destinations to share and get ideas. I would love, love, love to see someone at high school given the chance to shadow our First Minister for one week or one day each year, a set week celebrating Scottish Parliament and Scottish Education. I would definitely apply for that chance.

Most important of all I want to continue to see a Scottish Parliament that I am proud of, celebrating diversity, good manners and opportunities for everyone regardless of their background.

*Dionne Hossack, 17, South Lanarkshire*

# CHAPTER 6

# People-Powered Politics

FIONA DUNCAN

IN 1998 A Consultative Steering Group report, 'Shaping Scotland's Parliament', acknowledged the people of Scotland's 'high hopes' for the Scottish Parliament, and the opportunity

> to put in place a new sort of democracy in Scotland, closer to the Scottish people and more in tune with Scottish needs.

I was delighted to be asked to contribute to this book and in doing so, I called upon the help and wisdom of three inspirational young people with whom I have had the pleasure of meeting and working with in my role as Chair of the Independent Care Review.

The Independent Care Review only exists because children and young people with experience of what is referred to as the 'care system' challenged people in power about the care they had received for many years and how it *hadn't* met their needs. Worst of all, it had put them at a disadvantage for the rest of their lives in numerous ways.

Families, children and young people who have experience of the 'care system' are some of Scottish society's most marginalised citizens and are disproportionately affected by a wide range of Scotland's most challenging issues such as poverty, low educational attainment, unemployment, homelessness and poor physical and mental health.

Back in 2012, with incredible support from the charity, Who Cares? Scotland, a group of children and young people campaigned for change. They told their own stories about what it feels like to grow up away from their birth family, not to feel accepted or loved or to know their personal history; they described the frustration felt when day-to-day and life-changing decisions are taken about you that you are not able to influence or control.

These children and young people spoke to elected members in their local area, to their MSPs and to party leaders and gave evidence to the

Education and Culture Committee. One of those voices belonged to Thomas Carlton, who has been part of the Independent Care Review since it embarked on its 'Discovery' stage in May 2017, and who prior to this, was integral in making sure a review happened.

## Contribution from Thomas Carlton

2019 marks 20 years of devolution in Scotland. I remember being informed in my latter stages of primary school that our new, or reinstated, parliament would enable Scottish responses to Scottish need. It would not be until I was a few years older that I would understand what that meant in reality.

As someone with experience of care and of youth homelessness, I was intrigued to learn of divergent policy development in relation to responding to homelessness in Scotland, compared to solutions being forwarded elsewhere in the UK. Our internationally commended policy developments in relation to homelessness demonstrated a capability of the Scottish Parliament to bring elected representatives together to collaboratively work on constructing the Scottish solution to a particular need. Despite a change in administration, the shaping of the legislation was instigated by one government and then finalised by the next. This demonstrated to me that the Parliament could focus on the need of the electorate rather than the need to adhere to party ideology.

In 2012, I became aware of a courageous group of 21 care leavers who were utilising their own experiences of being parented by the state to influence the Parliament's thinking in constructing a new way forward. The young people's strength, and the elected members' flexibility in ensuring they were accessible, led to the passing of the Children and Young People (Scotland) Bill 2014. I sat in Parliament in February 2014 as the bill was passed and was shown that Scotland's Parliament was accessible to all of its citizens, including its most disenfranchised: children brought up in care who face indescribable challenges. Children like me. This legislation was underpinned by lived experience and extended the offer of support to this group of Scottish society. Even today it seems unbelievable to me what was achieved.

The courage demonstrated by those with lived experience, by sharing their stories, shaped the legislation and gave me permission to utilise my own lived experience of receiving care, and professional experience of working in the sector in driving more change for the care-experienced population. I provided evidence to the Education and Culture Committee in August 2014. This was the first time that I had spoken openly of my time in care. Prior to this, I had tried to conceal it in fear of the discrimination that I'd possibly experience in my early social work career. The work of the Parliament legitimised our experiences and made it harder for others to use those experiences in a way that might hinder my career.

The passing of the Children and Young People (Scotland) 2014 Act defined corporate parenting in Scotland. All those identified as corporate parents within the legislation, had to be mindful of their day-to-day working and ensure it did not impede upon the wellbeing of those with experience of care. Scottish Ministers were listed as corporate parents. At this time, I was a policy officer at a children's charity. We, with others in the sector and most importantly with people with lived experience, spoke of those seeking to govern as also seeking to become the most senior corporate parents in the nation.

In order for those prospective senior corporate partners to be adequately prepared for their new, or continued role, there was no protocol. In preparation for the 2016 Scottish elections, we lobbied those seeking to govern so that they would commit to listening to the people for whom they would have corporate parenting responsibilities. We asked, and evidenced the need, for them to commit to listening to a representative group of the care-experienced population, prior to forwarding policies or legislative change that could impact on the lives of those affected.

The need for this was demonstrated by the fact that on an annual basis, since the establishment of the new Parliament, policy or legislative changes despite lacking improvements for the outcomes of those with experience of care. This group of people continued to have some of the worst life outcomes in our society, in spite of the Scottish state having significant involvement in their day-to-day care. If this was to be different in any way, policy-makers would require greater reference points to understand what they could actually influence.

So, with the backing of the 1000 Voices campaign led by Who Cares? Scotland, care-experienced people were successful in securing manifesto commitments from all of the main political parties seeking to govern in Scotland 2016. These parties committed to ensuring they listened to the voice of lived experience when they assumed the highest offices in the land. This commitment was further realised in October 2016 when the re-elected First Minister of Scotland announced the commission of a 'root and branch review' of the care system.

* * *

Traditionalists might refer to what Thomas has described as grassroots activism or 'bottom-up' legislative change, but these expressions reinforce the hierarchy and position of decision-makers sitting at the 'top' and looking 'down'. Just as considering someone or a group as 'hard to reach' both 'others' the person or group and shifts responsibility towards them to be more reachable.

Instead of using language that insults the very people who public services are intended to serve, this different type of policy-making should be seen as in keeping with that 20-year-old 'hope' for our parliament. In creating legislation and policy, Scottish parliamentarians have an obligation to truly engage and listen.

Participating in a meaningful way in any legislative or policy consultation requires dedicated resources, such as time to review and settle on a response, and skills to craft this and ensure it is 'submitted' on time. This process lends itself to well-organised and resourced groups. Typically, these groups also hold power through their size, reach and often their brand, and therefore the policy consultation process lends itself towards a ruling class of those with the most members and the loudest voices.

Over the coming 20 years, our Parliament has a responsibility to organise itself in ways that ensures it is able to listen carefully to the voice of the Scottish people whilst inuring itself against powerful lobbyists. Better still, within the coming 20 years, and ideally sooner, the Scottish Parliament could aspire to reflect the people of Scotland in all their beautiful diversity, and not rely on process to achieve representative voice. That would be a huge step towards a truer version of democracy and the diffusion of power.

Despite the inherent power imbalance in how legislation has been made for decades, a group of children and young people who are, or had been, cared for by the state called for – and got – the Independent Care Review.

They challenged the First Minister, who listened and responded directly. Sturgeon made a promise to the children and young people seated in the front rows of the SNP party conference in autumn 2016, and more than this, she stated that the Independent Care Review would be 'driven by those who have experience of care'. That day, children and young people knew that they had been heard and received a promise that they would continue to be heard.

One of the people who has dedicated her life to change and was there at that very moment was Laura Beveridge. I knew Laura only from her TEDX Talk and from the coverage of the day of the First Minister's announcement. I then met Laura on my first day as Chair and have since had the immense privilege of working with her in her role as a Co-Chair. Her wisdom, compassion and determination give me confidence and inspiration.

## Contribution from Laura Beveridge

I knew injustice as a child but didn't have the language to express how I felt. I lived in a system that was designed to contain and control. As a homeless 16-year-old I had a choice to make – give up or try to change the system as a worker. However, as a worker, I felt as oppressed by the system as I did as a child. It broke my heart to see 16-year olds facing homelessness after leaving care, seeing children face isolation in their communities because children in care were labelled as 'bad'. I could see the continuing struggle children and young people had in accessing simple experiences like sleepovers with friends or keeping in touch with brothers and sisters and maintaining these vital relationships, because there wasn't enough staff to facilitate 'contact'. I had to speak out.

I found my care family through Who Cares? Scotland. A family of powerful campaigners who had already changed the law-making the Children and Young People (Scotland) Act 2014 happen. But we all knew that it would take much more than law to change the system. We needed Scotland to understand.

Being welcomed into the Scottish Parliament by all political parties as a result of the 1000 Voices campaign was an unforgettable experience. I, alongside many others with experience of care, asked MSPs to not only listen, but pledge that they would do all they could to transform the care system into a place to call home, a place full of love and hope. The campaign manifesto was subsequently signed and supported by all party leaders.

Care is something that not only cuts across all political parties, care is part of being human. We all deserve a place to call home and to be loved. On two occasions, political leaders gave us much more than their allocated time, they listened with care, and they signed with love. I believe they will act on the Independent Care Review recommendations because they know it has been driven by care-experienced people and they know this is about the rights and needs of Scotland's children. I firmly believe that the Scottish Parliament is a place for all of us and I am proud to be part of this movement that includes all who care.

When a 'root and branch review' of the care system was announced, it filled my heart with hope because I knew that it would be our voices that would drive the change needed and that Scotland was finally brave enough to do things differently.

To be part of the Independent Care Review is a privilege. The fact that it is independent and driven by voice of the care-experienced community feels meaningful and liberating. To be in a space where we are working alongside infants, children, young people and adults who have experience of care is an honour. We are listening, designing and learning in a new, exciting way that is so full of possibility.

What gives me hope is that a precedent has now been set. Finally, we do this together and, crucially, the voice of lived experience will continue to be heard.

\*\*\*

As Laura so eloquently describes, the Scottish Parliament, as the seat of the Scottish Government, is the place for those in power to listen. It is a place that young people and future generations should have a role within and a place with an open door.

Many of the children and young people involved in the Independent Care Review, due to their age, don't recall any of the controversy over the Enric Miralles design and the subsequent build costs. However, they often do appreciate its architecture and talk about the change from light to dark and back to light again as they navigate through what can feel like a warren. There is also an appreciation of the openness of the space immediately outside the building, and how it makes it easy to arrange to meet each other before going in, with some saying it is also the perfect place for a political protest. And I know now first-hand that the Parliament Café inside provides a good spot to sit and settle any nerves in advance of what might be to come.

It is interesting to reflect on the principal comparator that children and young people have – mainly television news coverage from the Houses of Parliament. This often shows Members of Parliament boorishly shouting at each other and rolling their eyes as they are seated directly opposite one another in the Commons Chamber.

The Scottish Parliament's Debating Chamber elicits praise as it is not obvious from the semi-circle formation who is 'against who'. Everyone faces in the same direction, towards the Presiding Officer, making parliamentary business appear less adversarial – Miralles' architecture encourages consensus and compromise.

Robust debate does require airing and hearing of a range of opposing views, but what is important in any argument is behaviour. The people of Scotland have elected Members of the Scottish Parliament to argue for us and can expect them to do so in a way that models good behaviour, that avoids an oppositional style and avoids the emergence of an antagonistic culture of political discussion. Clearly this aspiration remains a work in progress, but ideally one that will not take 20 years to achieve.

So, the design of the Scottish Parliament alongside the electoral system for the Scottish Parliament are in keeping with the aspirations of the Scottish Constitutional Convention (1995) that

> the coming of a Scottish Parliament will usher in a way of politics that is radically different from the rituals of Westminster: more participative, more creative, less needlessly confrontational.

This aspiration continues to feel very relevant for how we should tackle big issues over the coming two decades. In terms of the Independent Care Review specifically, this approach should inform how important decisions are made about what sort of Scotland we want all our children and young people to grow up in.

If Scotland is going to deliver against the National Performance Framework 'petal' that states 'We grow up loved, safe and respected so that we realise our full potential', Members of the Scottish Parliament have an obligation to embody characteristics that demonstrate love, safety and respect. And today in Scotland, there are conversations about putting kindness into public policy, so it is incumbent on our Scottish Parliament to create space that encourages consideration of others, openness of mind, generosity of spirit and empathy.

The findings and recommendations of the Independent Care Review are more likely to deliver what is needed, if our politicians are willing to support any changes to legislation based on the needs of the children and young people, and not political doctrine.

There is growing appreciation that by working together, policy-makers and citizens will make better policy, and approaches to making this happen are evolving. We have become very familiar with buzzwords like empowerment, collaboration, co-design and co-production. However, there are also real challenges with this, starting with the need to make absolutely sure that this is truly authentic and not a tokenistic exercise, or a passing fad. There are numerous examples of co-design and co-production being led by groups of expert people that have already formed their view on what any output should be. They unconsciously filter what is being heard, biasing any outcome and leaving those who thought they were being heard feeling used and with even less power.

This is clearly related to the earlier point about inherent power imbalances and vested interests. For the Independent Care Review, that includes some of the many custodians of the complex 'care system' with its multiple rule makers and decision-takers comprising of the state, charities and independent providers who deliver care right across Scotland.

There is an argument that the proliferation of reviews, inquiries, commissions and task forces etc. coming from the Scottish Parliament and Scottish Government could be seen as an indication of government absenting their responsibility for tackling the more complex challenges and passing the buck to another. When I raised this with a senior Member of the Scottish Parliament, she gave a challenging response to this, questioning the role of the voluntary sector as an active and vocal lobbying group that frequently demanded change for beneficiaries. She also rightly challenged how charities use their power, suggesting that many of the changes demanded would benefit the organisations as much as the individuals they represent. Although there is some truth in this, there are many charities that clearly state their obsolescence as the marker of greatest success.

It is no secret that the Independent Care Review's position is in support of the trend of the experts in policy-making being those who have lived experience. In the world of care, how it feels to be cared for must be a more important factor than the components of the system that is 'delivering' care.

It will be the clear and brave voices of infants, children and young people (and increasingly adults) with experience of the care system who will inform the Independent Care Review's understanding of what has to change.

The Independent Care Review has met with many infants, children and young people across Scotland. They have shared their stories about their experiences of care with a view to making things better now, and for future generations. Listening to the voices of its citizens is a critical part of any democracy; we listen to children in our families and so we must keep listening to children in care.

Every single day, the Independent Care Review strives to ensure the voices heard in every single discussion and debate reflect the people that best understand the 'care system' – those who have lived in it. This very deliberately goes beyond the First Minister's promise of 'driven by' with every conversation chaired by someone with lived experience and all significant outputs peer reviewed by people with care experience.

A part of the Independent Care Review's remit is to 'look at the underpinning legislation, practices, culture and ethos'. At the last count, the 'care system' comprised of 44 pieces of legislation, 19 pieces of secondary legislation and three international conventions. So, in terms of accountability and responsibility, as much of that labyrinth of legislation (not mentioning the associated policies and practice guidelines) sits with the Scottish Parliament, and all the associated committees that are organised to reflect the bureaucratic framework.

A truly ground-breaking approach to recalibrating how the Scottish Parliament works over the coming 20 years would be to create an environment that actually reflects how people live; that supports legislative reform that prioritises the population; and a move away from the current silos and systems riddled with bureaucracy – that would be transformational.

Meantime let's not underestimate the scale of the challenge ahead for the Independent Care Review. The current complex legislative landscape that makes up the 'care system' comprises of multiple decision-makers, each with their own set of rules, languages and timescales. Each part of this 'system' relies on data, evidence and analysis, all of which is intended to measure that aspect's success or failure. More often than not, none of this takes any account of the experience of life in the 'system'. Regulators, inspectors and auditors look at compliance, efficiencies and costs of delivery and not how it feels to have 'a sense of family. Of belonging. Of love. A childhood' – the aspiration of the Independent Care Review.

Everyone involved in the Independent Care Review cherishes its independence and it is this that will enable the First Minister's promise to be kept. Any outcome will need to be understood and respected across all political parties in order that the change that is so desperately needed can happen, without systemising, monetising or politicising our children and young people. Because the Scottish Parliament is unicameral and there is no revising chamber the parliamentary committees, those groups that reflect the balance of all parties, to do their job, to take evidence and to scrutinise, have a really important job to do.

On 14 March 2018, Kevin Browne-MacLeod, Rosie Moore and I represented the Independent Care Review and gave evidence to the Education and Skills Committee. That nerve calming café came in very handy beforehand. At the end of the session, Johann Lamont MSP said:

> For those of us who are a bit more hard-bitten about stuff, there have been a million reviews on a million issues in this parliament, but you have given us huge confidence that this is taken forward really, really seriously. And I think across whatever party people come from they will be hugely encouraged by what you have said.

That felt like an enormously positive outcome after what had felt like a grilling in a formal room. Many young people in care spend far too much of their young lives in austere rooms being talked about or at by 'experts' but as Rosie explains below – giving evidence to the committee was a very different experience to what she had expected.

## Contribution from Rosie Moore

Although I was pleased to be asked to represent the Independent Care Review at the Education and Skills Committee, I was very nervous at the prospect. I didn't know what to expect as I had never been to the Parliament building before and I thought it would be very formal.

We entered the room just as the previous session was ending, to get a feel for what it would be like. I initially felt very intimidated as there was a very large table and everyone around it seemed to be very formal and professional. However, as soon as the previous session ended, I was pleasantly surprised that everybody immediately relaxed and were very friendly towards each other. The committee members came over to us and introduced themselves to us and immediately put me at ease, explaining exactly what would happen next.

When our session started, I felt aware that I was the least professionally experienced person at the table. I was worried that I might feel embarrassed by not being spoken to as much as everyone else or would not know the answers to any high-level questions. However, in actual fact I was spoken to with equal respect and interest throughout the entire session. The committee members made me feel at ease and felt that I was genuinely being listened to. It was very empowering.

\* \* \*

In looking forward to the next 20 years, the Scottish Parliament will need to make sure it is equipped for Scotland's huge socio-economic challenges. Therefore, it must continue to think and act in innovative and authentic ways to ensure that as a modern parliament it enables its elected members to truly serve their constituents.

In deciding what the big issues are for Scotland, the Parliament must look to the views of the people it represents today – and in the future – and encourage respectful debate and protest. Tacking those big issues and making Scotland the best place to grow up will require the Scottish Parliament to work harder to represent the diversity of the people of Scotland.

The Independent Care Review knows that people who face the most disadvantage are also among those whose voices are least heard, who feel excluded and forgotten. So, the Scottish Parliament must place greater value on lived experience and ensure that those with the least power have their voices heard.

In addition to an open-door policy, a truly accessible and inclusive parliament has a duty to reach out to listen. Those who may be socially or geographically excluded from taking part must be given routes to contribute to or influence Scottish policy and legislation. An aspect of this must be investment in innovative digital platforms that are engaging, while ensuring that individuals are supported to take part in a safe way.

The recent strike that Scottish children led in order to challenge leaders to take action on climate change is a brilliant example of this, and I was encouraged to see political and public support of those young people taking a stand on an issue that really matters to them.

Members should strive to be role models for our young people and seek to work across parties to enact solutions and positive change for Scotland. This can only be done by really listening to people and being steadfast in the fight *for* the people – too often we see politicians caught up in the fight *against* each other.

Young people are more informed and have more potential for influence and activism than ever before. This should be nurtured, stimulated and appreciated. Trust is fragile and once lost is very difficult to earn back. So, politicians should seek to authentically interact with the people they are representing and avoid exploitative and tokenistic methods of engagement.

Members who strive to be true to the people whose votes gave them the mandate to serve must do justice to that position of power and should never take the trust invested in them for granted, instead continually earning and maintaining it through conduct that merits it.

The Scottish Parliament has a track record of endeavouring to lead in terms of not tolerating the poor conduct of its members in relation to racism, sexism and matters of integrity. The bar for accountability must be set high so that those who fail to reach it need to seek careers elsewhere.

Government has a role to play in challenging traditional models of power and encourage meaningful participation as it alone cannot make the changes required.

As Thomas, Rosie and Laura have described, the Scottish Parliament has listened and given them their rightful place in Scotland's highest political forum. Their expectations for what the Parliament does next are appropriately very high. So, I conclude by inviting all Members of the Scottish Parliament to commit to working with the Independent Care Review to ensure that the transformational change that is needed can be supported and implemented effectively. In doing so, my hope is that 20 years from now the voices of lived experience who have bravely led the Independent Care Review, will be honoured by a brave new Scotland that truly knows how to care.

CHAPTER 7

# Local Government and the Scottish Parliament

## Parity of Esteem?

ALISON EVISON

TWENTY YEARS AGO, when the Scottish Parliament was first elected, local authorities across Scotland looked forward to improved relations with central government. Relations between the old Scottish Office and local government had been tense and at times conflictual. The Convention of Scottish Local Authorities (COSLA) provided the Scottish Constitutional Convention with the secretariat and support in drawing up plans for devolution. Over 90 per cent of Scotland's local authorities played a full part in the Constitutional Convention's deliberations. The cross-party Consultative Steering Group (CSG) set up after the devolution referendum agreed key principles that should guide the Parliament in the years ahead which were welcome to local government. Sharing power, greater accountability, access and participation and the promotion of equal opportunities together suggested a major role for local government.

The establishment of a commission to consider relations between the Parliament and local government under Sir Neil McIntosh, former local authority Chief Executive, was even more positive. The McIntosh Commission reported shortly after the first elections to the new Parliament and made a series of recommendations that took notions of sharing power and accountability further. It argued that relations between central and local government should be based on mutual respect and parity of esteem and that relations should be informed by the principle of subsidiarity. Centralisation should only occur when the Parliament demonstrated the benefits and that subsidiarity should reach into our communities.

Parity of esteem recognised that no single institution had a monopoly of wisdom. It acknowledged that when it comes to delivering public services that local government has experience and expertise that is lacking at central government level. The importance of public and other bodies pulling together was deemed necessary.

There is no doubt that local authorities have enjoyed a close relationship with parliament and its various committees over the last 20 years. Local access to decision makers has been facilitated by the existence of the Parliament. Local government input to policy-making and the easy access to government ministers have ensured that the local government voice is heard. Local authorities shared in the increased expenditure that was a marked feature of the early years of devolution.

There have been many joint policy initiatives that have improved the quality of life of our citizens. COSLA worked with the Scottish Parliament and welcomed the passage of the Community Empowerment Act. We have also worked with Andy Wightman in his effort to translate the European Charter of Local Self-Government into law in Scotland.

Twenty years on, however, it is difficult to avoid the disappointment felt across local government that such high ideals and this hopeful start have been lost. There is still much co-operation in many areas but reflecting on these ideals at this 20th anniversary of the Parliament is an opportunity to assess progress, consider challenges that lie ahead and discuss how to re-imagine how these ideals and principles should be translated into practice.

Elsewhere in this volume, James Robertson notes the inscription on the wall in Holyrood drawn from one of Walter Scott's novels. Scott has one of Edinburgh's citizens wanting to be able to 'peeble them wi' stanes when they werena gude bairns' with the 'bairns' meaning politicians. While this should never be taken literally, accountability is important and the opportunity for citizens to engage with decision-makers is a hallmark of any democracy. But while Walter Scott's character was complaining that 'naebody's nails can reach the length o' Lunnon', it should always be remembered that the Scottish Parliament feels remote for most people in Scotland. The Parliament's efforts at outreach and engaging with the public are recognised but necessarily have limitations. In simple geographic terms, bringing power nearer to the people cannot be achieved by the Scottish Parliament alone.

## Parity of Esteem

Parity of esteem was based on the acceptance that local government, as the only other elected authority, had a legitimacy that matched that of the Scottish Parliament. It is true that participation in local elections has remained low but the argument that one institution's mandate is greater than another simply based on turnout would place Holyrood behind the House of Commons in esteem. We need to address low levels of participation in elections, and much else as discussed below, but there is ample evidence that people are more likely to vote if they perceive the institution as powerful. Empowering local government and ensuring that it is recognised as important in the lives of our people is an obvious next step in the development.

Mutual respect is essential if challenges that lie ahead are to be effectively confronted. COSLA jointly signed and launched the National Performance Framework (NPF) last June as part of this joint working. The NPF's ambitions for Scotland will only be achieved by working together and recognising that central and local government, along with the third and private sectors, mutually respect each other including, especially when we have our differences on how best to achieve these outcomes. The power sharing ambitions set out by the CSG subsequently adopted by the Parliament need to be extended beyond Holyrood.

The key sphere of local government has been absent in the consideration of parliament's principles. As the Parliament itself reflects on progress over the last 20 years and considers the future it would do well to amplify its founding principles and incorporate local government. Under these key principles on its website, the Parliament proclaims:

> Power should be shared among the Scottish Government, the Scottish Parliament and the people of Scotland.

To make this more meaningful, this should be amended to proclaim that in the next phase of its development,

> Power should be shared among the Scottish Government, the Scottish Parliament, *Scotland's local government* and the people of Scotland.

The language that is used in how we discuss politics can trap us into a mindset that is unhelpful. References to 'postcode lotteries' damages the idea of local accountability by suggesting that everywhere is the same and every community will have the same preferences and priorities. It is right that we learn from each other, as local government has always sought to do, and benchmarking to encourage improvement is important but we have to be careful not to assume that one-size-fits-all. Scotland is richly diverse and if our governance fails to reflect that diversity, we will undermine much that is celebrated in our communities.

## From Taken for Granted to Esteemed and Valued

There are matters best handled by parliament and others, by local government, and these need to be respected. But there is much that will be shared. Part of the problem in relations has arisen from a tendency for parliament and parliamentarians to ignore the boundaries between devolved and local government responsibilities. Members of the Scottish Parliament (MSPs) are rightly quick to complain when Westminster dares to trample on Scottish Parliament business. But Holyrood must always recognise that this also applies to its relationship with local government.

Of course, these boundaries are not fixed and should not be seen as walls that are guarded jealously. Our whole system would operate more effectively if we recognised our interdependence. It is inevitable that the elected MSPs will want to raise local constituency matters in parliament, including matters that directly come under local government. But greater care is required for parliament and parliamentarians to avoid further mission creep and consideration is now required to reverse that which that has occurred over a long period of time.

The gradual erosion of local government's status started from well before devolution, but it has continued under devolution. Local government in Scotland, and across the UK as a whole, lacks the formal entrenched status that exists in many countries. Formally, parliament had authority to impose its will on local government to the point that it could theoretically abolish all 32 local authorities. This theoretical power is, of course, unrealistic. It is worth remembering that much legislation and policy would be meaningless without local government's ability to implement and deliver policies. Herein lies one of the problems. Much that local government does is simply taken for granted. Without local government those services would grind to a halt.

The status of local government should be recognised formally. An obvious way of doing this would be to adopt the Council of Europe's European Charter of Local Self-Government. Scotland is one of the most centralised countries in Europe and implementing this charter would do much to alleviate this. The charter was ratified by the UK Government in 1998 but was never been translated into law. The Scottish Parliament has the opportunity to translate its provisions into Scots Law recognising the principle of local self-government. It would embed local authorities' right to share power, outline local governments' powers and responsibilities and parliament would require their consent before any amendment. It would allow greater autonomy for local authorities to determine their internal workings, ensure that local authorities are adequately empowered financially to deliver the services for which they are responsible and allow local government to work in partnership with others.

While it might be contended that legislation of this sort might be easily overturned by parliament at any future date, it would at least provide some protection and signal a new approach that built on the McIntosh recommendations. It would also require primary legislation to alter the balance in the relationship and meet the McIntosh principle that centralisation should only occur when Parliament has demonstrated its benefits.

There has, of course, been progress in crucial areas. Clause 7 of the Islands Act 2018 includes the 'duty to have regard to island communities'. An equivalent duty to have regard to the diverse local communities should exist in law for local governance more generally. The Islands (Scotland) Act 2018 also includes a provision for island councils to make additional powers requests (Section 15 and 21), allowing these local authorities to ask that additional functions, duties and responsibilities should be transferred to that authority. These provisions could be rolled out across Scotland.

Each generation or so, we have re-formed local government and our tendency has been to do so in a top-down manner. In this process we have tried to iron out differences and remove diversity. As we move forward, we should reflect the same thinking that led to devolution by recognising diversity and that will mean addressing asymmetries. Devolution is different in Scotland, Wales and Northern Ireland. Even the nomenclature differs with the Scottish Parliament, Welsh National Assembly and Northern Ireland Assembly. And, of course, there is no devolved government for England. Asymmetry has been embraced in one sphere but appears to cause deep concern when applied to local government.

No two parts of Scotland need have exactly the same system of local governance. This is not about creating a messy system of governance but reflecting Scotland as it is, rather than how it should be, in a bureaucratic mindset. Local government should be set up in such a way that it can work for local communities.

We are more likely to achieve the same outcomes for our people by permitting greater diversity in our governance arrangements than by imposing uniform structures on diverse communities. This may seem paradoxical but is easily explained. Just as no two people are the same, no two communities or places are the same: what is needed to ensure that individuals' and communities' prospects and life chances improve, cannot be expected to be achieved through uniformity.

## Disempowered Individuals and Communities

A current example of co-operation between the Scottish Government and local government has been the review of local governance. This review is a shared endeavour. It was designed together; evidence has been gathered by both spheres and has been considered jointly. The reform proposals that will emerge should be jointly owned. The first phase of this reflects the importance of increasing participation and engagement, alluded to above. We have come a long way from treating our people and communities as mere recipients of public policy. The tendency of doing things for, and to, people is now recognised as paternalistic and has severe limits. It disempowers people and communities.

As noted above, low turnout in elections will occur when people feel that there is no point in voting. When it comes to individuals, research shows that mental and physical health are affected by the sense of being disempowered and alienated. This will apply to communities as well. The public health agenda on which, again, the Scottish Government and local authorities are working constructively together acknowledges the central role of people and communities.

For some years now we have sought to engage with people and communities. The Scottish Parliament has played a noble part in this, constantly considering how best to engage with the public through its committees and outreach. Initiatives such as participatory budgeting have proved valuable both in terms of lessons learned, but also in allowing local priorities and preferences to be heard in the allocation of resources. The first phase of the local governance review was designed to hear the voices of communities across Scotland. The second overlapping phase focused on governance arrangements.

The key message that has emerged from local government in this review has been clear: our people and communities need to be empowered. This idea will be familiar to the founders of the Scottish Parliament. The CSG referred to the need to create an

> open, accessible and, above all, participative Parliament, which will take a proactive approach to engaging with the Scottish people – in particular those groups traditionally excluded from the democratic process.

The case for a Scottish Parliament was more than about Scotland's constitutional status but about a different kind of politics. There was a desire that our politics and society should be more engaging and participative at the outset of devolution. We should use this anniversary to reflect on this and consider how best to advance this idea into the future.

The form empowerment takes will vary across Scotland. But local government has identified three interlinked forms of empowerments that are applicable across all of Scotland: community empowerment; functional empowerment; and fiscal empowerment. Each of these empowerments depends on the other.

## Community Empowerment

Empowering our communities will require us to take the ideas that led to the Scottish Parliament's establishment a stage further. Our diverse communities include communities of place and of interest. Communities overlap and people will feel part of more than one community and at times may identify more with one than another. Many communities have the 'social capital' necessary to engage fully with decision-makers and some may want to see power and resources devolved deeper into the communities beyond local government while others may be content to know that their voice is heard. Creating cohesive, confident and resilient communities requires that we spread involvement more widely and especially involve individuals and communities largely left behind by our current systems. This cannot be done by parliament on its own.

The right to be involved in decision-making is not common across all public services. Local authorities have a better record than most, but much more could and should be done in all spheres. Public engagement is socially patterned with vulnerable and marginalised groups all too often left out of decision making. We cannot hope to close the attainment gap in education without hearing and acting in response to these voices. We cannot expect to close any gap by ignoring those who have been left behind. The paternalist approach that assumes that professionals know best, or even that elected members can speak for everybody, has proved unsuccessful. The notion that men could represent for women, that property owners could speak for those without property and that older voters could represent young voters has long since been discredited. The idea of local self-government means that we need to build the capacity to participate and engage across our communities. This links with the common understanding across the sphere of government that we must tackle inequalities.

One of the key challenges in the years ahead will be to consider the relationship between representative democracy, in the form of MSPs and councillors, and participatory democracy. Social media and digital opportunities mean that how politicians engage as elected representatives has changed and will likely change further. Long gone are the days when being elected every few years and holding regular surgeries was sufficient. We have experimented with a variety of forms of public engagement. Both local government and the Scottish Parliament would benefit from sharing and learning from this experience.

Such changes will create a more vibrant democracy but will not be achieved without cost. This includes costs in time but also financial costs. Some savings should accrue by more collaboration across public services at a local level, but we should not pretend that empowering people and communities can be done on the cheap or within existing local authority budgets or current structures. Embedding community empowerment requires not only that specialist staff are employed to assist in this, but that empowerment is mainstreamed amongst all officials and elected members.

While there is much support in principle for empowering communities, too often this is thought to be something for others to do. But all institutions – the Scottish Parliament included – need to consider how best to ensure that we engage with our communities taking advantage of opportunities afforded by emerging technology.

## Functional Empowerment

Our governance structures were created in a different era. Devolution was an important development. We now need to have the same focus on Scotland's internal governance, and how the Parliament relates to this, as we have spent considering relations between London and Edinburgh. The McIntosh Commission's report needs to be dusted down and those recommendations which were not implemented, considered and updated.

Holyrood should review the powers it has accrued not only from Westminster since the advent of devolution, but also those it has sucked up from local government in the last 20 years. Creeping centralisation has occurred over time. The principle of subsidiarity, that central government should only have responsibilities which could not be performed locally, was supposed to guide relations with local government. Acquiring local powers should have only occurred when a demonstrable case could be made for centralisation. This has not happened. Not only should this McIntosh recommendation be enshrined in law, but the Parliament ought to consider how many of its existing competences and resources would be better decentralised to local government. Just as local government is learning to devolve to local communities, so too should the Scottish Parliament and Government learn to devolve to local government.

Our institutions often operate in institutional silos and while Community Planning Partnerships have offered a way forward there remains much more that could be achieved. Parliamentary Questions and parliamentary accountability encourage this silo approach at national level, and this flows through into local governance. For too many public services the lines of accountability lead upwards in a centralising silo manner and ignore lines of accountability into our communities. It will not be easy, but we need to give more time to thinking about how Scottish Government responsibilities at local level relate to local government.

Ministerial announcements have tended to apply policy uniformly and might achieve an immediate headline but may be less successful in the longer-term objective of achieving improved outcomes. Whether it is health, education or any range of policy areas, the tendency has been to set aside public funds for some purpose that requires all local authorities to graciously accept and fall into line. This diminution of local autonomy is not working for our communities.

## Fiscal Empowerment

The advent of the Parliament has done nothing to reverse the decades long trend towards centralising funding for public services. Ring-fencing funding has become an increasing feature of public finance that owes more to the desire for claiming credit at central government level than for good policy-making. But ring-fencing resources is an example of the centre assuming a monopoly of knowledge and expertise. Local financial autonomy has been squeezed over time, reducing local government in some respects to local administration. Once more, the lessons of the evolution of devolution over the past 20 years should guide us over the next 20 years. The Scottish Parliament was essentially a spending institution at its inception and was occasionally criticised for being fiscally irresponsible in having no concern for how the money that it spent was raised. That has changed and continues to change with the new fiscal powers that it has acquired.

Local government has seen its grant from the Scottish Government cut in real-terms, but it is not only seeking to go cap in hand for more money, but it is rightly arguing that it should have the means of raising more of its own money. It seeks fiscal responsibility as the corollary of fiscal empowerment, just as the Scottish Parliament has gained fiscal responsibility with fiscal empowerment.

## Conclusion

Reflecting on the last 20 years, it is clear that the Scottish Parliament has had a significant and positive impact on Scottish society. The experience has taught us much. As we look to the next 20 years, we should consider the relationship between the Parliament and the government institutions in Scotland more broadly. Lessons can be drawn from the relations between London and Edinburgh which could be applied to relations between the Scottish Parliament and local government. Sharing power, increasing accountability, access and participation and promoting equal opportunities remain important principles and apply across all of Scotland's public institutions.

*Dear Scottish Parliament...*

The Scottish Parliament has been active for 20 years, and in this time, much has been greatly improved overall in Scotland. However much more could be done, especially by adhering to the views of the youth of today who will soon be the ones making decisions for parliament and shaping the country in entirely new ways. Having been born just four years after the Scottish Parliament was formed, I have been lucky enough to grow up in Scotland in the early years of the Parliament and though great steps have been made to improve the country, there is still work to do, particularly for those who will soon be the representatives in the Parliament.

As a 17 year old growing up in a small island in the north of Scotland, the work of the Scottish Parliament has been fundamental in shaping my beliefs and views. From the change from Standard Grades to National 5 and Highers, to issues such as accessibility on boats to the islands, my life has been greatly impacted by the Scottish Parliament. I believe that for the Scottish Parliament to continue its work, its inclusive approach such as allowing 16 year olds the vote must be carried on into the future. Scotland became the first country to have an all-inclusive compulsory education for the LGBTQ+ community, and though this is fantastic, I believe that more could be done to protect the rights of minorities. Education into LGBTQ+ relationships has recently been a topic of debate. That this is even up for debate is outrageous. Everybody should have an understanding of their peers and if this was addressed in every child's secondary school then discriminatory based bullying would be more successfully eradicated. This could potentially be done by inclusion of those 16 and 17 year olds in parliamentary debates, First Minister's Questions and committee work – the direct views of the youth are critical in understanding who they are coming from.

I also believe that youth mental health continues to be overlooked. Mental health issues are still not discussed in depth, making people unaware of the signs of problems that could prevent fatalities or irrevocable damage. As technology has rapidly increased and become more accessible, so too has the number of children being admitted into therapy and counselling. Although social media is critical in elections, spreading information, communication, the internet has also quickly evolved negatively. As the link between media perpetuated stereotypes of young people and old people alike is undeniable, and though it is impossible to fully contain this, the repercussions must be addressed by parliament. If MSPs addressed this, along with other issues raised by today's youth, with young voices not only heard but *listened to* then Scotland will become a nation which strives towards acceptance and pride of all. This is, I believe, achievable in the next 20 years.

*Ellie Gauld, 17, Orkney*

## CHAPTER 8

# Scrutiny and Transparency

### CAROLINE GARDNER

Open the doors! Light of the day, shine in; light of the mind, shine out!

THE OPENING LINE of Edwin Morgan's poem written for the opening of the Scottish Parliament building vividly captures three of its founding principles. The Parliament should share power with the people of Scotland and the Scottish Government; the Government should be accountable to the Parliament, with both accountable to the people; and the Parliament should be accessible, with an approach to policy and legislation that embraces all levels of society.

The principles sought to embed scrutiny and transparency at the heart of the new Parliament, along with a wider sense of openness – a people's Parliament. That ambition extended to the Parliament's role in making Scotland's public finances open and accountable to the people of Scotland.

The post of Auditor General for Scotland was established as part of those arrangements, together with Audit Scotland, the body created to report to the Parliament on devolved public spending. As Auditor General since 2012 I've had a ring-side seat as the public finances have undergone remarkable change, allowing Scots to take more responsibility for our country and how it works.

We've seen some important developments – new financial powers, a new parliamentary budget process, and a distinctive Scottish approach to public services, intended to put improvements for individuals and communities front and centre rather than playing a numbers game. But the stakes are also much higher than they were in 1999, and there's more to do to make those principles a reality.

When it was established in 1999, Holyrood was almost entirely a spending parliament. The Scottish Government's budget for 2000–01 was £18.3 billion, with more than 90 per cent funded via the block grant from Westminster and just 8 per cent raised in Scotland (through non-domestic rates). The budget had very little relationship to Scotland's economic performance and the Government had little scope to increase it. The Parliament's main financial role was to approve the Government's spending proposals, set out each year in the draft budget, and scrutinise how the money had been spent at the end of the year.

The Scotland Acts of 2012 and 2016 devolved a range of taxes, including full control of non-savings, non-dividend Income Tax rates and thresholds; the proceeds of the first 10p of the standard rate of VAT; and taxes on land and buildings transactions, landfill, air travel and aggregates. It also introduced new borrowing and reserve powers and devolved 11 social security benefits worth around £3.3 billion each year.

These changes, now well on the way to being implemented, will increase the amount of revenue raised directly in Scotland from around £4 billion in 2015 to £22 billion in 2021; from just 10 per cent of the budget to more than 50 per cent. The remaining 50 per cent will continue to be funded through the block grant from Westminster.

We've seen a shift from a spending Parliament to one that needs to balance spending with revenue and manage much greater complexity, volatility and uncertainty. Scotland's relative economic performance will directly influence the amount of money available to the Government for spending and investment, as well as driving the level of spending on areas like social security, with all the opportunities and risks that brings.

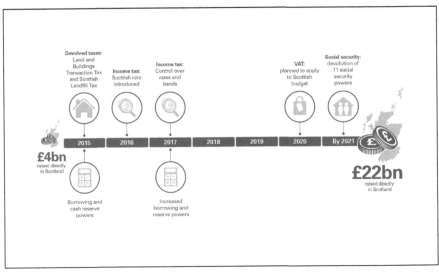

Source: Audit Scotland

It's hard to overstate the importance of these new powers. They give the Scottish Government incentives to grow Scotland's economy and more scope to raise money to pursue its own policies. Financial sustainability has never been more important. And the Parliament needs to be able to scrutinise how the new tax and spending powers are being used to ensure the decisions taken by government are thoroughly tested and properly challenged. In particular, it needs to be able to move on from scrutinising each year's budget in isolation to examining the sustainability of the public finances as a whole, in a way that's entirely new.

But it was increasingly clear that the Parliament's budget process was no longer fit for purpose. Its founding aspirations for greater openness and involvement hadn't been fulfilled, and the need to make decisions about tax raising and social security with long-term implications meant the problem was acute.

A group established to review the budget process found several weaknesses. The timing of the Scottish budget meant that scrutiny was squeezed into a few weeks around Christmas – too short to focus on more than a few headlines, the political hot potatoes and the current controversies. This became a particular problem from 2016, when the Chancellor announced that the Autumn Budget would become the UK's main fiscal event, allowing even less time for the Scottish Government to understand and manage the implications for its own budget.

Parliamentary scrutiny was also too narrow, with a focus on changes from year-to-year rather than a longer-term approach, and little evidence of significant change to the government's spending proposals as a result of the budget process. Any changes that were made tended to be the result of deals between political parties instead of committee scrutiny, and to involve additional funding rather than changes to spending plans.

A new, more strategic, approach with a year-round approach to budget-setting, scrutiny and evaluation was recommended. It replaced a narrow focus on movements in budget lines year-on-year with a wider examination of what's being spent, what's being achieved and, crucially, whether it's providing value for money. The new approach builds on what some committees – especially the Health and Sport Committee – were already doing, seeking to extend good practice and reshape budget scrutiny. Parliament and government agreed, and the new budget process was introduced from 2019–20.

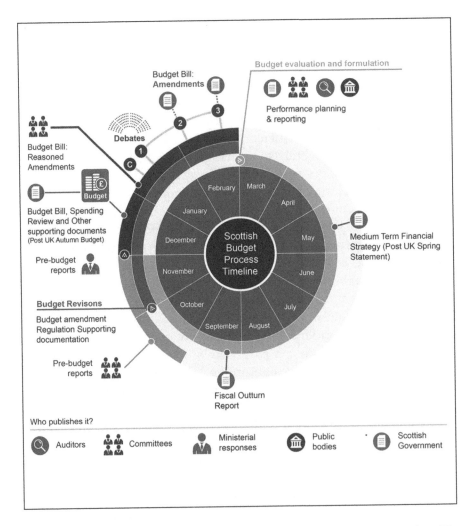

A more strategic approach means joined-up thinking across the different components of the budget – revenues, spending, borrowing and reserves – and understanding how they interact with each other and with economic performance. Should Scotland increase sustainable economic growth by raising the tax rates under its control and investing the revenues in economic development, education and childcare? Or should we reduce tax rates with the aim of unleashing entrepreneurial activity in the private sector and increasing tax revenues that way? These are inherently political questions, and the Parliament needs to be able to play its part in shaping and challenging the Government's plans.

These choices will set the direction for the public finances and determine how resilient they are, but we will also need short-term flexibility. For example, when tax revenues fall short of the forecasts, as they're bound to do on occasion, the Government has three options: cut spending, use the Scotland reserve or, in very limited circumstances, use its revenue borrowing powers.

The Fraser of Allander Institute has estimated that a difference of just 0.3 per cent in the rate of income growth between Scotland and the rest of the UK will lead to a difference of £50 million in the Scottish Government's revenues. In good years that represents extra money to spend, but in lean years the Government will have to close the gap in its spending plans. And that's just the first year; if the difference continues, a windfall or a black hole will rapidly build up. All of this will require the Government to set out its financial policies and scenarios over a much longer period than in the past, and the Parliament to scrutinise them effectively.

Parliamentary committees' roles have also changed, using the extended budget evaluation and formulation stage to look back at what's working, look ahead to the issues and challenges and consider what this means for future budgets in their areas.

They need to look closely at the Government's planning and performance reporting, and that of the public bodies; what they're aiming to achieve, how they intend to do so and whether their plans are being delivered. The focus should be on evaluating the outcomes expected from public spending, bringing together financial information with evidence about performance, and examining how this is informing policy development and decision-making.

For example, the Government has a long-standing vision for the NHS, based on providing much more care in people's homes, and other homely settings, rather than in acute hospitals. There's a widespread consensus that this is the right way forward as the population ages and more of us are living with long-term conditions that need to be managed rather than cured. But to make it a reality, the Parliament and its committees need to be able to scrutinise the Government's plans for change and what progress is being made.

At the moment this is difficult. The budget documents don't yet provide enough information about how the Government expects to improve outcomes for patients by reducing reliance on acute hospitals. And NHS performance information is incomplete, focusing heavily on waiting times for hospital treatment; we know much less about the performance of vital services like general practice, community nursing and social work that help avoid unnecessary hospital admissions and get people safely home afterwards.

Committees have a role to play but the Government also needs to fill the most important data gaps, particularly information on activity and demand in primary care. This will enable committees to scrutinise government plans and influence the content of the budget proposals up front, through discussion and dialogue at the committee and by setting out their views in a pre-budget report. It also enables broader-based parliamentary scrutiny, asking bigger questions about effectiveness and impact over time and across portfolios.

Of course, the budget is just one point in the cycle of scrutiny and transparency; what happened in practice is just as important in terms of accountability to parliament, especially with greater volatility and uncertainty.

Audit is central to this process, and Audit Scotland is generally seen as one of the successes of devolution. It audits more than 200 bodies across the public sector on behalf the Auditor General and the Accounts Commission, providing independent assurance that public money is spent properly, efficiently and effectively.

Our performance audit reports on major public services like the NHS, education and childcare tend to attract the most attention, but our work goes much further. We also publish an annual audit report on each public body, and I report to the Parliament on matters of public interest. These reports are a valuable source of information and insight to government and the Parliament, but repeated reports on the Scottish Police Authority and NHS Tayside, for example, suggest that government can be slow to respond to audit findings and recommendations. The Public Audit and Post-Legislative Scrutiny Committee has expressed frustration that the same issues come up again and again.

Beyond the budget cycle, one more aspect of parliamentary scrutiny hasn't lived up to expectations; the Parliament's legislative process. It was designed to ensure that the financial costs of bills are taken into account – getting the budget estimates right at the outset should have meant better planning and decision-making and underpinned post-legislative scrutiny.

In practice it hasn't worked well. For example, the success of police reform was hindered by the fact that the costs were taken from an outline business case prepared without adequate baseline data; a full business case was never prepared, and the cost information wasn't updated during parliamentary scrutiny of the bill.

More recently, the Fuel Poverty Bill introduced by the Government in 2017 provides a new definition of fuel poverty and sets a target of reducing the proportion of Scottish households in fuel poverty to no more than 5 per cent by 2040. A SPICe briefing recognises that the new definition is a genuine attempt to identify and support households in financial hardship, but it also notes that there's no estimate of how much reducing fuel poverty is likely to cost.

So, there's room to improve the transparency of Scotland's public finances and strengthen Parliamentary scrutiny. The new budget process, when fully implemented, will go a long way towards this, but the changes required are ambitious and there's a lot still to do.

The Government needs to improve its financial reporting. Factual content needs to be separated from the political narrative in the budget document; and there should be a consistent approach to the presentation of financial data. Figures need to be comparable year-on-year; and how the Scottish Government is funded – the fiscal framework – needs to be clearer.

We've seen some welcome developments, including the publication of the Government's first medium-term financial strategy and fiscal framework outturn report, both of which provide important new information about the longer-term picture. But there are also some areas that don't yet measure up. For example, the 2018–19 budget set out the block grant adjustments that would result from the methods preferred by both the Scottish and the UK governments – which are critical to the budget and are due to be reviewed in 2021 – but this information was omitted from the 2019–20 draft budget without explanation.

Local government funding is another area that needs to be presented more clearly, particularly given the role that councils play in delivering national policy priorities. Changes in funding are difficult to decipher, leading to claims and counter claims that generate confusion. The Government needs to continue to make the budget document simpler and more transparent, so that the Parliament and its committees can scrutinise it effectively.

There has been little visible progress on another central element of good financial reporting, a Scotland-wide account pulling together the whole public sector. This might sound like something that's of interest only to auditors and other anoraks, but in Scotland's new fiscal world that overall picture is vital.

The global financial crisis highlighted the importance of a thorough understanding of the public sector's assets and liabilities and the key risks to its financial position. The Spanish Government, for example, lacked comprehensive information about the total level of borrowing across all parts of the public sector. When tax revenues fell as a result of the economic shock, local government bodies were unable to meet their debt repayments, leading the Spanish Government to step in to service their debts and maintain essential public services. We all want to avoid a situation like this, especially since future global events will now have a much more direct impact on the Scottish economy and the money available for public services.

The Scottish Government's consolidated accounts are the main vehicle for accountability to parliament. They are important in their own right, but they don't include important elements like local government borrowing and public sector pension liabilities. These are significant omissions: the pension liabilities on the NHS and teachers' pension schemes, and the net liability on the local government pension funds, amount to more than £100 billion; while local government borrowing exceeds £15 billion. This is information that MSPs urgently need to take a longer-term view of public finances.

It's a strange anomaly that, although the Scottish Government doesn't produce its own public sector consolidated account, its figures are included in the UK Whole of Government Accounts. These accounts are recognised as being among the most comprehensive published by any government and are increasingly used to improve decisions about public sector assets and liabilities. It's hard to argue that there wouldn't be at least as much value in producing the equivalent picture for Scotland, particularly at a time of significant change and uncertainty. The Permanent Secretary committed the Scottish Government in November 2016 to publishing a consolidated account for Scotland and the commitment has since been repeated; it's now time to demonstrate real progress.

Of course, taxes and public spending are a means to an end, not an end in themselves. The next step is to focus on the impact of spending decisions on people and communities. As Bruce Crawford, Convener of the Finance and Constitution Committee, said during the Parliamentary debate on the new budget process:

We need to move from a position of judging success based on the number of police on the streets or the number of nurses in our National Health Service to one that involves measuring the sustainable outcomes that are achieved by public spending in Scotland.

The Government has taken some major steps. The National Performance Framework setting out the priorities and outcomes that the government wants to achieve is now established in legislation and has attracted international attention. I've no doubt that this is the right way forward, but in practice it's often hard to see its impact. Detail and delivery matter; it should be possible to follow the line of sight between the National Performance Framework and every strategy, plan and funding decision, but that's not always the case.

There are some early priorities. For example, the Government's infrastructure investment plan doesn't articulate how each investment is intended to address the priorities in the National Performance Framework. A clearer understanding of the intended benefits and outcomes would help the Parliament to make trade-offs between, for example, transport and lower carbon infrastructure, early years and higher education, or primary and secondary healthcare.

And making a reality of the outcomes approach means embedding it in policy-making. Let's look again at healthcare. The outcome that the government is working towards is a nation that is healthy and active. It's a truism to say that health is about much more than the NHS – improving health also means investing to improve housing, poverty, work and communities, all of which the Parliament has some levers to change. But government announcements and parliamentary scrutiny tend to focus on narrow issues like NHS funding and waiting times, rather than considering how best to use those levers to improve health outcomes. That means looking at the evidence of what works, planning what action the government and public bodies need to take and putting money and other resources behind it. Given the time it will take to improve the outcomes that matter most, it also means being clear about how progress will be measured along the way.

And most of all it's about people – the people who provide public services and the people who rely on them. In our work at Audit Scotland we hear every day from nurses, doctors, social workers and other public servants who know they could provide better care but feel frustrated by the organisational barriers and boundaries that get in the way. Those barriers are never deliberate, but a failure to truly focus on the outcomes we want to achieve makes it harder to identify and tackle them.

A couple of examples from people we've spoken to in the course of our work on health and care help to illustrate the challenge. First, The Food Train is a charity that started out in Dumfries, pairing older people with neighbours who volunteer to buy their groceries while doing their own shopping. As well as fresh food, the older person gets some extra company and the pair get to know each other better. Over time the pool of volunteers has grown to include, for example, young people with learning disabilities who also benefit from helping develop skills that support them into work.

The benefits are clear, and the charity has grown to cover many parts of Scotland. But there's a real frustration among staff and volunteers alike that the help they could offer is limited by the way health and care services work. For example, if the older person is admitted to hospital for any reason, their GP practice is often reluctant to let The Food Train know when they are due to be discharged. This means that the volunteers are unable to make sure there's food in the fridge, or pop in to make sure the person is OK when they get home. It's hard to see who benefits from this, but nobody seems able to change it.

Second, we often hear complaints that police officers are often the first to respond to vulnerable people, especially those with mental health problems, but in many ways the police are ideally placed to provide the first response – they work across Scotland 24 hours a day, and they often get to know their communities better than anyone else.

The problem isn't that police officers are often the first to respond to vulnerable people, but that they can't arrange the help and support those people need. That puts the police in a difficult position, it perpetuates an approach to health and care that isn't flexible or responsive enough and, most of all, it lets down some of the most vulnerable people in society. If police officers, health and care staff, or social security advisers were given the freedom to do what's needed to improve outcomes for the people they serve, public services would work quite differently and we'd be much closer to becoming a 'healthy and active' nation.

We'll only see that sort of transformation by opening up and involving people in decisions about public services and public spending, from the Parliament to communities and individuals. That openness will also be essential if we're going to be able to tackle the challenges facing Scotland – managing our new tax and spending powers; reshaping health and care services to meet the needs of an ageing population; and making a reality of inclusive growth in the context of globalisation and technological change.

Some of the building blocks are already in place through the Community Empowerment Act and the Open Government commitments, and the review of the budget process stressed the importance of involving people in the decisions that affect them. The Commission on Parliamentary Reform also made a number of recommendations for opening up the Parliament in line with its founding principles. But there's scope to go further, in line with the Government's aim of a Scotland that is innovative, pioneering, inclusive and creative.

There's no one-size-fits-all approach, but Scotland is in a great position to experiment as part of its commitment to improving outcomes. There's increasing evidence of the effectiveness of participative budgeting (PB), which has strengthened communities and increased wellbeing in Brazil by making public services better and more accessible. There's also evidence that the participation of people from low-income groups has influenced the way money is spent – in the city of Porto Alegre this meant prioritising sewer and water connections, which rose from 75 per cent to 98 per cent of households.

Closer to home, PB is a central pillar of the Community Empowerment Act. The adoption of PB is now under way in Scotland, but challenges of culture, capacity, politics, legitimacy and sustainability have so far limited the opportunity to make a substantial difference in the lives of citizens and communities.

Citizens' juries and other forms of deliberative democracy are also promising. Their role in shaping the debate on abortion rights in the Republic of Ireland, helping to develop a degree of consensus a question that has historically been deeply divisive, has attracted a lot of attention, and they've been suggested as a way of healing the divisions over Brexit.

All this really matters. The Parliament and the Scottish Government have laid some strong foundations for effective scrutiny and transparency but there's still a lot to do, with big risks and tremendous opportunities. We've got the chance to develop a world-class approach to public finances and public services, learning from the best globally and tailoring it to Scotland's particular circumstances. Let's make the most of it.

*Dear Scottish Parliament…*

Being a bisexual young woman, I am proud of the Scottish Parliament for legalising gay marriage in 2014. I feel that the importance of legalising gay marriage cannot be underestimated. Not only did it, finally, give gay people the right to have their union recognised by law, I believe that it had a huge effect on the fight against homophobia as well.

I grew up in a family that was covertly homophobic. I never felt that I would be in danger if I came out, however, I didn't feel I would be accepted. In fact, my grandmother's younger cousin was, essentially, ostracised from our family for coming out as gay. I believe that the legalisation of gay marriage in 2014 sent a clear message: homophobia is not welcome in Scotland. Following, the legalisation of gay marriage, my family have, for the most part, seen the error in their ways. They have seen how gay people were persecuted since, essentially, the beginning of time for something beyond their control. They have seen how their homophobia has ruined the potential to develop bonds between people. They have seen the damage homophobia has on an individual's mental state – how it can break a person. Even my grandparents went to Pride this year! If you had told me that, a year ago, genuinely, I think that I would've laughed in your face.

I want to see the Scottish Parliament continue to lay down the bricks – to build a country that is both inclusive and diverse I want to see more representation within the Scottish Parliament. I want to see diversity in every form. I want better education. I want children to know that it's okay if you aren't attracted to the opposite sex. I want them to know that they're not wrong. I want them to know they're not alone.

Specifically, I want better social education. I want education about the variety of types of relationships. I don't want to hear about, solely, heterosexual relationships. I want to hear about homosexuals, bisexuals, pansexuals, demisexuals, asexuals… the list goes on and on and on. I don't want people to be put in boxes. We are not this or that. We are a multitude of things.

Each and every human being is different and lies on a unique point on an infinite spectrum of humanity. That is why the human race is a wonder. Because no one of us is the same. Because the things that make us stand out are the things that wonderful. The legalisation of gay marriage, back in 2014, was a start. But more needs to be done so that everyone (regardless of who they are) has equal rights and opportunities. I look forward to the day in which this dream becomes a reality.

*Emma Cook, 15, Edinburgh*

CHAPTER 9

# Raising Taxes

## Charlotte Barbour and Moira Kelly

AT THE HEART of whether the Scottish Parliament is well placed to tackle the big issues facing Scotland is the need to fund its activities. The Parliament's powers over taxation have evolved significantly over the last 20 years. The funding has changed from that in 1998, when the Scottish Parliament was almost entirely reliant on the block grant from Westminster with very limited tax raising powers, to its position today where it has powers over a basket of taxes and collects around half its budget through those taxes.

Devolution of tax powers has introduced new opportunities, but also new complexities with many moving parts to manage. There is the politics of managing perceptions, to which all tax law-making bodies are subject. There are also specific features of the devolution settlement, such as the interaction with UK taxes, the benefits regime and the UK budget, and understanding how the block grant adjustments work. Both sets of factors can make it more difficult to scrutinise tax policy effectively. And, although the debate around Scottish taxes by both politicians and the wider society has changed significantly over the last 20 years, there remains scope for further public involvement.

This chapter looks at the challenges the Parliament faces in scrutinising tax policy and reviews examples of where it has worked well and how this can be improved in the future.

## Background

Following the establishment of the Scottish Parliament, devolved powers relating to taxation were minimal. Tax policy remained outside the Scottish Parliament's legislative competence except for two measures. One was local taxes: Council Tax and business rates. The second was a power for the Scottish Parliament to vary the basic rate of Income Tax by up to plus or minus three pence in the pound. This power was never exercised by the Scottish Parliament.

Scotland's tax powers further evolved through the Scotland Acts of 2012 and 2016, which provided the Scottish Parliament with authority over a range of taxes. These 'Scottish taxes' cover a variety of allocations of responsibilities and powers, in relation to specific taxes, including:

'Full' devolution, where total responsibility for the tax is devolved to the Scottish Parliament, such as taxes on land transactions and on disposals of waste to landfill and, in the future, air passengers and aggregates;

'Shared' or 'partial' devolution, which involves joint responsibilities split between the UK and Scottish Parliaments. This applies to Income Tax, which is currently the only shared tax;

'Assigned' taxes, where the tax remains a UK tax with full responsibility for legislation and administration sitting with the UK authorities, but some of the tax revenue is allocated to Scotland. The first 10 per cent of the standard rate and the first 2.5 per cent of the reduced rate of VAT is assigned to the Scottish budget each year from April 2019.

The measures have been designed so that Scotland's economic performance may influence the amount raised through the new taxes. It also means that the country benefits (or risks) if the amounts raised are more (or less) than budgeted.


## The Evolution of Scottish Taxes

Scotland Act 1998:
Scottish Parliament established
With responsibility for Scottish Variable Rate (SVR); Council Tax; business rates

Scotland Act 2012:
Land and Buildings Transaction Tax (LBTT) (2015)

Scottish Landfill Tax (SLfT) (2015)
Scottish rate of Income Tax (a single rate) (2016–17)
Scotland Act 2016:
  Scottish Income Tax (full control of all rates and bands) (2017–18 onwards)
  VAT assignment (April 2019 onwards)
  Air Departure Tax and Aggregates Levy – in the future

The Scottish Government has had to adapt to deal with the evolving tax powers, both at a political and operational level. In the 2018 Scottish reshuffle, the establishment of a ministerial-level position with responsibility for tax policy was a recognition of the increasing prominence of the devolved taxes. Similarly, the machinery of government is also responding to these changes.

## What Has Worked Well?

The Scottish Parliament has introduced Scottish Income Tax rates and thresholds. It has also used its tax powers to create a number of transaction taxes and established:

a tax authority to be responsible for the administration and collection of the devolved transactional taxes (LBTT and SLfT);

an independent Scottish Fiscal Commission;

tax tribunals for hearing devolved tax disputes (LBTT and SLfT).

## Scottish Income Tax

Following the Scotland Act 2016, the ability to set in full both the Income Tax bands and rates, for specified types of income, rests with the Scottish Parliament but all other aspects of the tax remain with the UK and are administered by HMRC.

The Parliament can, for example, set the amount of Income Tax that Scottish residents pay on income from a job or pension but other aspects of the tax regime, such as setting the tax-free Personal Allowance or deciding how and when tax is paid on income arising from savings or dividends, remains with the UK Parliament.

The direction of travel with five bands and a more progressive and distinctive charging structure was set in 2018–19. With this structure, the profile of Scottish Income Tax has been raised as the differentials between Scotland and the rest of the UK have increased across thresholds and rates, and from one year to another.

The proposals are set out in the Scottish Government's budget each year, with MSPs required to pass a Scottish rate resolution. However, parliamentary arithmetic – with no one party commanding an overall majority – has led to accommodations having to be reached by successive Scottish Governments with other parties, behind closed doors, to allow the measures to be passed. This has resulted in less open discussion in committee and the Debating Chamber. For example, following negotiations to ensure the support of the Scottish Green Party for the 2018–19 Budget, the higher rate threshold for 2018–19 was amended down from the proposed £44,273 to £43,430.

## New Devolved Taxes

With effect from April 2015, taxes on transfers of interests in land and on disposals to landfill have been devolved. The new taxes being LBTT and SLfT respectively. Scotland is now responsible for raising its own income from these sources and the Scottish Parliament has introduced the necessary legislation to do so. Similar measures will apply in due course to UK air passenger duty when the fully devolved Air Departure Tax (ADT) comes into effect for flights leaving from Scottish airports. The Air Departure Tax (Scotland) Act 2017 received royal assent on 25 July 2017, however, these proposals remain in the hangar due to EU state aid issues which have prevented the tax from being implemented.

## Scottish Primary Tax Legislation – Enacted by Holyrood

Land and Buildings Transaction Tax (Scotland) Act 2013
Landfill Tax (Scotland) Act 2014

Revenue Scotland and Tax Powers Act 2014
Land and Buildings Transaction Tax (Amendment) (Scotland) Act 2016
Air Departure Tax (Scotland) Act 2017
Land and Buildings Transaction Tax (Relief from Additional Amount) (Scotland) Act 2018
Administering Devolved Taxes

As well as legislating for the new devolved taxes, the Scottish Parliament has enacted the Revenue Scotland and Tax Powers Act 2014. In very broad terms it provides the following:

The establishment of Revenue Scotland as the tax authority in Scotland, with the responsibility for the collection and management of the devolved taxes;

The relationship between the tax authority and taxpayers in Scotland and the relevant powers, duties and rights;

A structure for resolving disputes, providing for internal mechanisms within Revenue Scotland by way of internal review or participation in mediation. Failing this, a taxpayer may take their case to an independent tax tribunal;

A general anti-avoidance rule.

## Setting the Tone

The Scottish Government has set the tone around its new tax powers. Adam Smith's four canons of taxation have been adopted in its approach to taxation, namely, certainty, convenience, efficiency and burden proportionate to the ability to pay. Following the 2016 Scottish parliamentary election, and the appointment of a new Cabinet Secretary for Finance and Constitution, there has been a subtle change in approach with the increased prominence of additional objectives such as the need to raise funds, bring accountability, support other policies such as economic growth and redistribute resources.

The Scottish Parliament has taken a strong stance on tax avoidance.

The Revenue Scotland and Tax Powers Act provides for a Scottish General Anti-Avoidance Rule (SGAAR) that has been designed to differ from the UK and to apply in a wider range of circumstances. In the UK tax legislation, there is a General Anti-Abuse Rule with abuse being considered to be more narrowly defined than 'avoidance'.

## The Challenges in Scrutinising Tax Policy

There are challenges for the Scottish Parliament in its new role of raising a significant part of its revenue from Scottish taxes. These include the need to learn about both devolved and reserved taxes, the detail required in tax legislation and how to prevent unwanted tax avoidance.

## Learning Curve

As with any new measure, one of the challenges is in facing a learning curve and, if a power to levy taxes from citizens is introduced, there are particular obstacles to learn about along the way. For example, legislation to levy a tax needs to be precise; what exactly is to be taxed and when, and so on. Drafting defects in the legislation result in either an inability to raise the tax, or what might be viewed as an unfair tax that is charged on unexpected transactions, as has happened with the Additional Dwelling Supplement (with questions around the definition of who should be chargeable) and the subsequent need to revise the provisions. The devil, as always, is in the detail. And with self-assessed taxes there needs to be a compliance regime, which is usually based on penalties for non-compliance. Penalties, however, can lead to a sense of antagonism among taxpayers. For the legislators, getting the right balance can be difficult and most of the cases taken to tribunal so far have been over penalties that have been viewed by taxpayers as excessive and unfair.

And, while Scotland is taking more control over its tax raising and, hence, its spending, devolution is not necessarily a pathway to simplicity: more laws generally lead to complication rather than simplification. And tax complication, in turn, leads to the public not being able to understand their taxes, leading to potential disengagement and lack of compliance.

## Tax Avoidance

In recent years, there has been a drive by politicians to clamp down on what is viewed as 'tax avoidance'. Clearly, there is a desire that taxpayers should operate within the spirit of the law and not avoid what was intended by the legislators but there can be challenges in fully understanding the contributory factors. On the one hand, seeking to pay less tax may be 'tax avoidance'; on the other, it may be a taxpayer simply using the legal options available or tax incentives offered. Some of the challenges facing our parliamentarians in relation to the Income Tax powers include:

Learning about the interactions of different taxes and which tax levers are devolved or reserved;

Evaluating the levels of risk around potential behavioural reactions to tax measures;

Appreciating that, if a tax is 'competitive' and, say, the rates are reduced relative to those in the rest of the UK or rates increased, this introduces incentives to reduce (or avoid) tax. Differentials encourage tax planning.

There needs to be an understanding of how the different taxes across the UK and Scotland interact and the scope for behavioural responses to any changes in taxation. This is particularly so in relation to Income Tax where some, but not all, aspects are devolved. Income Tax is one of the three main sources of government revenue, the others being National Insurance (NIC) and VAT. Both Income Tax and NIC can be viewed as 'expensive' by taxpayers and employers and are consequently politically sensitive.

Any taxpayer who views a tax bill as an unwanted cost may seek to minimise this cost and so divergent rates across Income Tax (Scottish, Welsh and UK), Corporation Tax and Capital Gains Tax lend themselves to tax planning behaviours, such as business incorporation by an individual who wishes to be paid in dividends rather than a salary. Arguably, the political focus on 'avoidance' versus 'abuse' misses the point that there is a wider category of taxpayer behaviour responding to changes in tax law that is not quite strong enough to be categorised as either abuse or avoidance but can nevertheless affect revenues.

Challenges remain for the Scottish Parliament. These include evaluating the exposure to tax avoidance and recognising that the responsibility for the quality of the tax system lies with Parliament. Clear, good quality legislation is needed.

*Example: Sole trader versus company tax position, which exchequer benefits?*

Sole trader – Income Tax and NIC, Mrs Brown, Scottish taxpayer 2018–19

Mrs Brown's business has taxable profits of £43,430. As a sole trader (or as a partner in a partnership business), she pays Scottish Income Tax and UK National Insurance.

Mrs Brown's top rate of Income Tax is 21 per cent. She also pays UK NICS Class 4 at 9 per cent and Class 2 NICS at £2.95 a week (£153.40 per annum).

If Mrs Brown earned an additional £1 or more, the Income Tax on this income would be paid as Scottish Income Tax and received by the Scottish Government.

Company – Brown Ltd – owned by Mrs Brown, Scottish Taxpayer 2018–19

If Mrs Brown runs her business through a limited company and takes out all the £43,430 profit, with a salary just below the NICS threshold and the balance as dividends, she *would have no earnings liable to Scottish Income Tax.*

The amount paid out as dividends would be after Corporation Tax had been paid at 19 per cent. The dividends would be taxed at the UK zero-rate and then the dividend basic rate of 7.5 per cent.

None of the Income Tax paid would reach the Scottish purse as dividends and savings are not devolved.

*If Mrs Brown generated an additional £1 or more, the Corporation Tax and dividend Income Tax would be paid to the UK exchequer.*

## Accountability

Scottish parliamentarians need to get more involved in the development of the legislation. For example, turnout in the Debating Chamber for debate on the Revenue Scotland and Tax Powers Act 2014 was poor. Proper parliamentary scrutiny and open debate are also impacted by the cross-party accommodations which are agreed behind closed doors.

In addition, Parliament has responsibility for holding HMRC and Revenue Scotland to account to ensure that the legislation is being correctly implemented and followed and that enough guidance is made available to the public.

Active scrutiny is not helped by the Finance and Constitution Committee's remit being wider than tax and at a time when constitutional matters are taking up so much parliamentary time. As the Parliament evolves from being mainly a spending institution to one where tax is required in order to fund spending, it would be helpful if there was a tax committee.

## External Constraints

Whilst it may appear as though there is significant control of Scottish revenue raising, the practical realities may be limited, and more so than anticipated at first sight. There are practical limitations in the assignment of 'Scottish VAT': it does not offer direct controls over the amounts collected; revenues from the fully devolved taxes LBTT and SLfT are relatively small; the devolved taxes of ADT and the Aggregates Levy are on hold due to EU state aid issues; and the potential to have an Income Tax that diverges from the UK rates and bands may be constrained by both political considerations and potential behavioural changes. The headline of having control of around 50 per cent of revenues has significant practical restraints around it. Indeed, the shape of the devolution settlement (the interaction of what is and is not included) is a major limitation. (This is exemplified by the earlier incorporation example but also by the interaction with NICs, credits and benefits.) Regardless of these limitations, parliament should still endeavour to scrutinise the aspects over which it has control especially as this will be of less interest to third parties.

At present there is a very small window of time between the UK and

Scottish budgets. Improved communication channels between Westminster and Holyrood, which admittedly are getting better, would also assist in giving more time for scrutiny of proposed new legislation and the impact of planned measures emanating from the UK Government.

## A Relatively Small Tax Base for Income Tax

Scottish taxes do not sit in isolation – they are interwoven within the UK tax regime and there are connections and constraints which this imposes. This is another instance of the learning curve; parliament needs to be aware of these interactions when carrying out their scrutiny.

One example is the Personal Allowance, which is set by Westminster and applies to all UK taxpayers. The effect is that a significant proportion of the Scottish population are lifted out of Income Tax (44.6 per cent in 2019–20), in turn making the Scottish taxpaying base smaller. There are 2.5 million Income Taxpayers in Scotland and the average annual salary is estimated to be £25,000. Furthermore, in 2019–20, 7.7 per cent of Scottish adults (351,000 in absolute numbers) will pay a higher rate and 16,000 adults (0.3 per cent) will pay the top 46p rate. Potentially, taxpayers liable at the higher tax rates may be more mobile and thus could potentially cease to be liable to Scottish Income Tax. Whilst many believe in a progressive tax system, there are constraints and challenges in the size and shape and potential mobility of the Scottish Income Tax base which needs to be factored in when developing tax policy.

## For the Future...

A clear articulation of the Scottish approach to taxation would be helpful. The Finance and Constitution Committee is to be applauded for its inquiry, 'A Scottish Approach to Taxation', which began in 2016. However, at the time of writing, the inquiry – which remains listed under the 'current business' of the Committee on its website – has not taken evidence since 2017, presumably as the weight of its other responsibilities has taken hold.

Building in differentials between tax systems may lead to concerns that this opens the way for tax planning or avoidance and so there may be a tendency to opt for the same or similar measures. But it does not bring a distinct approach, nor may it necessarily be best suited to longer-term Scottish interests, so such decision making should be made against a considered framework. Scottish tax policy should be more than a 'cut and paste' with a few tartan bits.

Tax policy principles should include an articulation of when Scottish policy is to be distinctive and when it might follow UK measures and the role of tax reliefs. It should analyse the main drivers: to collect revenue, support economic growth or encourage certain behaviours. It should also have clear public messaging.

## Public Understanding

A recent poll shows a lack of understanding among the general public as to which Parliament is responsible for specific tax policies. As public engagement and understanding can lead to greater compliance, work is required in educating the population on the operation of Scottish taxes. Hopefully this should lead to widening participation in this area.

In the main, tax is seen as a cost and is considered by both business and individuals in any evaluation of whether Scotland is attractive. To inform such decision-making, there needs to be clear explanations of how the various 'Scottish taxes' work. There is also a need to consider the holistic or cumulative effect of the different taxes, such as Income Tax, Council Tax bands, and LBTT, where the impact on taxpayers may be cumulative (and not forgetting the impact on benefits). Public messaging around this, and which relates to the spending side of the equation, should be high on the list of priorities. It is important that existing Scottish taxpayers understand and support their contribution to public finances; it is equally important that the overall amount, and its purpose, is clear to those who may wish to move to Scotland.

## Processes Could Be Improved

The Scottish Government has been adapting to the changing tax powers (eg the subtle change in approach since 2016 and the establishment of a ministerial-level position with responsibility for tax scrutiny). However, given the wide ambit of the minister's portfolio, this might not allow sufficient time for the consideration of Scottish tax policy and its interactions with UK taxes.

The Parliament has powers to introduce legislative changes, either by means of primary or secondary legislation. To date, tax changes have tended to be introduced by a mixture of both primary and secondary legislation. This is especially so when new legislation is enacted and subsequently amendments are introduced. For example, LBTT was introduced by a stand-alone act but, since its commencement in April 2015, there have been several changes to it (using a mix of primary and secondary legislation), including:

A new charge to tax – Additional Dwelling Supplement;

A new relief – First-Time Buyer Relief;

Removal of anomalies – for example around group relief.

Unfortunately, legislation loses clarity if its measures are split between primary legislation and sets of secondary legislation. It is far easier to review and confirm provisions if they are grouped together.

A further disadvantage of secondary legislation is that it only changes the law from that point on. Although retrospective changes to the law are not normally wanted, when attempting to correct an error in the drafting of the law (for example LBTT group relief) then legislation with a retrospective effect may be preferable.

There is no regular process for bringing forward and considering such changes and it would be helpful if there was. This would assist in ensuring parliamentary time would be set aside for scrutiny. It would also provide an easy route for error corrections or reliefs rather than by, as at present, requiring a separate act or piece of secondary legislation. The introduction of an annual finance bill would lend itself to this process. Enhanced scrutiny should hopefully lead to the need for fewer future corrective amendments, making the whole process more efficient.

Going forward, there should be a clear rationale behind the split of measures between primary and secondary legislation (especially as the latter undergoes less parliamentary scrutiny).

As noted above, the Scottish Parliament could introduce a tax committee with members who develop specialist taxation expertise, particularly in relation to shared and devolved tax powers. This would ensure that time would be set aside for scrutiny and its members would be able to develop their tax expertise.

## More, New Taxes…

In Scotland there is scope to introduce new devolved taxes. The mechanism for doing so is set out in Section 80B of the Scotland Act 1998. Section 80B(1)(a) provides that the monarch has the power, by Order in Council, to specify 'a tax of *any* description' as an additional devolved tax. The Order must be made with the agreement of both the UK Parliament and the Scottish Parliament. The power has been exercised once so far, in the Scotland Act 1998 (Specification of Devolved Tax) (Wild Fisheries) Order 2018. Other suggestions put forward include a tourist levy, a vacant land tax and a charge on disposable cups. Such suggestions need robust public debate before proceeding. There are a number of issues to consider before seeking to introduce a new tax, including:

What are the objectives of a new tax (to raise money or to encourage or discourage certain behaviours)?

Should responsibility sit at Holyrood or with local authorities?

Will local tax raising create funding inequalities between local authorities?

Would hypothecated taxes be more palatable to taxpayers?

What taxes might fit the bill?

How would this interact with existing taxes (both Scottish and the rest of the UK) and benefits?

Suggestions for new taxes so far are unlikely to raise significant sums and they lend themselves to being set and administered at a local level by the local councils.

Council Tax and business rates are areas where the Scottish Government has much more autonomy and policy has been less fettered by interaction with other UK taxes. Revisiting these taxes could allow policies to evolve around progression and support for business, although perhaps with tension between the two goals.

## Scotland: A Centre of Excellence?

The Scottish Parliament has various possibilities open to it and, looking to the future, an ambition of making Scotland a centre of excellence in devolved taxes should be carefully considered. Excellence requires long-term strategic thinking. Surely this laudable ambition should be worth the concentrated effort required.

We look forward to the next 20 years.

# CHAPTER 10

# Twenty Years of Devolution

## Small Steps Towards Equality, But We Need Big Leaps

### Talat Yaqoob

IN ITS 20 years, the Scottish Parliament has had some success in being a global leader on equality, diversity and inclusion. The very creation of the Scottish Parliament building was to indicate the start of a more inclusive and accessible democracy. A modern parliament was created with the Debating Chamber built into a semi-circle, supposedly to encourage collaborative debate rather than the seating of Westminster, which invites opposition back and forth in a more adversarial manner. The timings of debate were scheduled to allow parliament business to be completed by 5.30pm and a crèche for visitors; the only parliament in Europe to have such a facility. However, whilst the aesthetics of the parliament may have developed with inclusion in mind, the equality created (or not) by the policy-making is dependent on the decisions made by those within it.

Through devolution, Scotland has the power, and to some extent has taken the opportunity, to set a clear and tailored path in education, health and its justice system. Within all of these policy areas lie chances to tackle deeply entrenched inequality. Some interventions have been pursued which have made a difference to peoples' lives. However, whilst recognising the limitations of a devolved settlement, which excludes legislative power over key areas such as immigration, equalities and employment, there are still ways in which Scotland's progressiveness is yet to dive beneath the surface to create the policy interventions needed to make radical change for those furthest away from access to power and opportunity.

## Who Makes the Decisions?

Multiple efforts have concentrated on the representation of who gets to make the decisions. In 2018 the Gender Representation on Public Boards

(Scotland) Act was passed, making it a legal obligation for public bodies to have 50 per cent women on their boards. Scotland is the first, and currently only part of the United Kingdom with such legislation in place. Women use public services disproportionately more so than men, so it makes sense to ensure that at least half of those making the decisions are women. The Scottish Government appointed its first 50/50 cabinet in 2014, which was applauded across the world and has funded the leading 'access to politics' programme which provides resources and financial support to disabled candidates enabling them to participate in local and national elections on a more level playing field. However, in reality, these efforts have yet to translate into a diverse looking Scottish Parliament. The number of representatives with a declared disability actually decreased in the 2016 election and the number of women elected remained static at 36 per cent. Most staggeringly, there is yet to have been a woman of colour MSP in the 20 years of devolution. This inequality permeates from the Scottish Parliament and into our society, where not one of the editors of Scottish newspapers is a woman and a mere 7 per cent of senior police officers are women.

Across politics, there is growing consensus for legislated candidate quotas. Indeed, in the years leading to devolution, a movement led largely by trade union women pushed for 50 per cent of those first seats taken in parliament to be reserved for women. That campaign may not have won, but it did create impetus for political parties to pursue women candidates and change their tactics. This led to a high of 40 per cent women MSPs in the first sitting of the Scottish Parliament, a substantial step change from Westminster, however in the years since, rather than achieving further progress, the proportion of women in the Scottish parliament has decreased since 1999. It is for this reason that the campaign for 50 per cent representation has been re-formed and has received more support than ever before.

However, for there to be real access into politics regardless of race, gender, disability, sexuality or class, there must be a transformation of the culture within the Scottish Parliament itself and politics in a wider sense. Currently, the expectations demanded of candidates renders the process of election essentially inaccessible, particularly for disabled candidates and those with caring responsibilities. If they were to manage through that process to becoming an MSP the pace, demand and round-the-clock nature of the work becomes another set of barriers for those who do not have the financial means to have assistance in all other areas of their lives (particularly those areas of our lives stereotypically and wrongly, assumed to be the work of women). Finally, the phenomenon of social media has changed the face of politics, making anonymous and hateful critique the norm for all. Women and specifically, women of colour, receive a disproportionate, violent and frightening level of abuse via social media, as revealed through Amnesty International UK's 2018 report. In order to create a worthy politics that individuals feel safe to be involved in, there needs to be tougher, technologically advanced and more vigorous attempts to tackle bigotry through these platforms.

Pursuits of representation are necessary in order for there to be lived experience around the decision-making table (producing better decisions) for society to have faith that the democratic process is fair, and that the powerhouse of Scotland reflects their lives and beliefs. Good policy-making comes from representative democracy, yet we cannot wait for representation in our chamber to finally come around for good policy to be implemented. At the current rate of change, it would take another 50 years for there to be fair representation of women in the Scottish Parliament.

There is no denying that the participatory culture within the Scottish Parliament differs from that of Westminster, the level of access and public engagement is lauded as one of the signature ways in which Scottish politics works; a 'Parliament for the people' as it was called upon inception. However, despite the relatively small size of the population of Scotland and this idea of access, those influencing the decisions of the Parliament whether through campaign groups, third sector organisations or lobbyists remain an exclusive and elite group of people. Often white, university educated, working within wider politics or policy research and disproportionately male. This becomes apparent by simply checking through those giving evidence to the Scottish Parliament's committees. We need to open the doors wider to influencers that go beyond those known and recognised within Scottish politics. We need to hear more and directly from the social care worker, the single parent, the immigrant, the nurse or the cleaner. A Parliament that is for the people, includes and takes seriously the voices of all the people.

## Every Policy Comes with Equality Consequences

There is no policy area under devolution that does not influence the progression or regression of equality of society. When we talk about equality and diversity, we should not and cannot be referring to some isolated policy agenda. It should be front and centre of all policy decisions being made; this is meant to be the rationale behind equality impact assessments, however this is rarely the case, as these assessments often fail to dig deeply enough into the implications of a policy to assess what real life impact it may have on different community groups. A high level of competence and knowledge around sex, gender, race, disability, migration, sexuality and class should be an expectation of those making Scotland's decisions and developing systems. A decision about the funding of policing, does not simply have a consequence on something as direct as the number of police officers, it has an impact on communities, the level and quality of support available to victims, and it has an impact on how decisions are made and why they are made in the justice system. A policy decision on primary education does not simply impact a curriculum, it can have an impact on access to support for children with additional learning needs or it may have an impact on the workload and wellbeing of teachers. There are equality and diversity consequences in every vote, every debate and every piece of legislation.

To review how far we have come on equality, we can look at some of the decisions which have been taken over the last 20 years and where we have failed to make the shift desperately needed. There have been ways in which Scotland has used its devolved powers to set a different course for the people of Scotland. The fully devolved area of education lends itself well to a review of equality implications. One of the most recognised policy decisions since devolution was the refusal of the Scottish Government to follow Westminster by introducing tuition fees for students. In January 2019 it was announced that Scotland had reached record numbers of students from deprived backgrounds entering first degrees. However, a refusal to introduce tuition fees has not in itself been the answer to widening access for students from poorer backgrounds, up until this year, the data on widening access revealed that Scotland has stalled in these efforts and remains behind England.

Furthermore, despite not paying tuition fees, Scottish students still leave university with significant debt, according to Scottish Government figures the level of debt accrued by students has increased by 75 per cent in the last decade. Across colleges, the Scottish Funding Council's data reveals a decrease of around 143,500 students between 2007–08 and 2016–17. Again, reviewing this through the lens of equality and diversity reveals that this decrease is largely in part-time students and disproportionality women and potentially older learners and those looking to re-skill or upskill whilst working, to give them access to more opportunities. Taking a look across further and higher education, we see the equalities impact and unintended consequences of decisions made.

However, some worthy gains have been made within education from early years to degree qualifications. Most recently, the success of the Time for Inclusive Education (TIE) campaign must be acknowledged, which fought hard for LGBT inclusive education to become standard in all state schools, making Scotland a world leader. Another leading initiative in education has been the introduction of gender action plans across universities and colleges, a public and funding dependent target of at least 25 per cent men or women in courses where there is a significant gender under-representation by 2030. For example, at least 25 per cent women studying engineering or computing and at least 25 per cent men studying nursing or teaching. These are necessary and positive steps, however underneath them needs to come efforts to challenge attitudes across society and accountability across education over implementation. In the case of tackling representation on gender segregated courses, the number of women studying computing, despite efforts, has fallen by 11 per cent since 2012. In a time where fourth generation technology is changing the face of the labour market, we cannot afford decline and to further exacerbate women's chances of future employment.

When it comes to fairness in education there is still so much to do. Actions need to be taken create classrooms free of gender bias, and indeed stereotyping of any kind; do more to support pupils living in poverty and give them a fair chance to excel; tackle the attainment gap which is most prevalent in schools in working class areas across Scotland.

To this day, sex (and most importantly consent) education is still not mandatory in all schools. At a time when the #MeToo movement is exposing allegations of sexual harassment from Hollywood to Holyrood, it is imperative that children growing up today understand their right to say no and equally understanding what 'no' means. Whilst we often make comparisons with Nordic countries with similar population sizes and democratic processes, we also need to take inspiration from them and pursue and invest in equality in similar ways. That includes at those moments where we feel discomfort. That discomfort is often a sign of a privilege or advantage coming into plain sight when an unequal status quo is finally being disrupted.

## Looking Through an Intersectional Lens

In recent years the term 'Intersectionality' has come into the lexicon of the Scottish Parliament. Coined by Kimberlé Crenshaw in the late 1980s, it was originally defined as the intersecting and multiple discrimination women of colour experience – sexism and racism. Since then it has come to be used as a way of describing any and all multiple discriminations being faced by an individual or group; classism and disabilism faced by a working-class man and wheelchair user or Islamophobia, racism and sexism faced by a black, hijab wearing woman. Whilst it may be considered a minor step toward progress for Scotland to be using this term, we are several steps away from intersectional thinking becoming the norm and genuinely understood in terms of political and policy change. Little to no meaningful disaggregated data exists to tell us about the lives of people experiencing multiple discriminations, whether it is labour market data or crime reporting. The very basic information on the experiences of those with living under the pressure of multiple inequalities is unknown. Without information, we can't make evidence led policy. When we do not deem it critical to collect and publish data, and count people's lives, we risk making assumptions about and excluding groups of people from Scotland's progress. Intersectional data collection, intersectional understanding and policy-making is the key to speeding up the pace of change on equality in Scotland.

Across Scotland there can exist an attitude that we are naturally more inclusive or welcoming. There is an idea of 'Scottish hospitality or friendliness' however, this notion can mask the reality of discriminations faced by individuals or groups. In March 2019, Amina Muslim Women's Resource Centre surveyed Muslim women in Scotland finding that nearly two-thirds had experienced or witnessed Islamophobia hate crime. Just one example of how far we are still to go to become 'one Scotland'.

According to the Council for Racial Equality and Rights (CRER), between 2000 and 2013, the number of murders with a 'known or suspected racial element' in Scotland was higher than that of the rest of the UK. Whilst hate crime reporting statistics tell us that there is a decrease in the number of reports of racially aggravated harassment, this does not consequently mean that racism is on the decrease. Far from it, with the rise of anti-immigration rhetoric and right-wing ideology across the world, we cannot be complacent. Instead Scotland could be using its powers to set itself aside from a rising tide of normalisation of hatred and othering.

A Race Equality Framework was launched in 2016 setting the tone on the delivery of racial equality in Scotland for the next 14 years. The framework is ambitious and sets objectives across a number of areas including, crucially, the justice system and education. It is still in its early stages, and whilst there is an acceptance in it that race and gender intersect to create a 'double discrimination', the actions delivered as a consequence of the framework need to go beyond mere acceptance. Instead the objectives must be bold in what is expected by government, local authorities, public bodies and employers as a consequence of intersectional thinking.

Going forward, to do right by black and minority ethnic people (BAME), women, migrants, disabled people, carers, LGBTQI+ and working-class people, these intersections need to become front and centre in Scotland's race equality efforts. Similarly, Scotland's Fair Work Action Plan was released last year, with the aim of supporting Scotland 'to be a fair work nation by 2025', yet there is little mention of the impact of institutionalised racism on the employment chances of the BAME community. A conscious effort is needed across all areas of society and across all institutions in Scotland to reflect on how racism plays out in their systems, in their decisions and their everyday behaviours. Simply writing an equalities policy or including faces of colour in the photos of your most recent publication is not solving racism, it is covering tracks. Instead reflection at both an individual and organisational level is required, with those in the Scottish Parliament leading the way.

A group which is too often forgotten when we talk about equality and diversity are unpaid carers. Left behind by swathes of policy-making which remains reserved and overlooked in the spaces in between. Despite the acknowledgement of the rapidly ageing population of Scotland and the awareness of the increasing caring responsibilities which often fall on the shoulders of women (particularly working-class women), when we talk about caring, we still assume 'parents and children'. This is then reflected in the decisions we make.

It is right that considerable investment is made in free childcare (although this investment still does not go far enough), however investment in those providing round-the-clock care for their elderly parents or disabled relative whilst being unpaid has not received the attention and policy interventions it deserves. One in ten in Scotland are providing some form of unpaid care to the value of over £10 billion per annum. Whilst some of this can only be resolved through a fair and functional welfare system the majority of which remains reserved to Westminster, further interventions which include mental health support for carers, investment in social care and improved housing and transport policy, can and must be pursued within the devolved settlement Scotland has now, otherwise we deeper entrench the very inequalities so many in Scotland are working hard to eliminate. The devolution of some social security powers provides an opportunity to do things differently. There has already been focus on ensuring Scotland's approach is one built on dignity and respect, but to embed dignity and respect requires a truly transformed system with those furthest away from power and wealth at its core.

This anniversary of the Scottish Parliament, should rightly, give us pause to reflect on whether the vision of devolution has been realised. Equality and diversity must be embedded in every aspect of process and every brick of the building of the Scottish Parliament. The starting point of any legislation passed in its Debating Chamber must be fairness for those most marginalised. By starting from there, and by including the voices of those who are marginalised and experience daily discrimination (whether that be based on their sex, gender, sexuality, race, class, disability, religion or otherwise), can we create policy which will have the positive impact we seek. Equality and diversity are frequently used as buzzwords to insert into a strategy or paper – but they need to be a living, breathing element of Scotland's politics and, with that, be a central part of how we hold to account the decisions taken by our Parliament.

Having a Parliament nestled in Arthur's Seat in Edinburgh has, without a doubt, had a positive impact on equality and diversity efforts across Scotland. We have been world leading on period poverty, on LGBT inclusive education, on equal marriage and on improved domestic abuse legislation. All of this should give us pride in our politics, but self-congratulations cannot shadow the deep-seated inequalities which remain. There are possibilities which are yet to be explored, and in the pursuit of fairness and equality, every avenue which can improve people's lives must be at the very least considered.

These are the responsibilities of those who have the privilege of sitting in the seats of the Scottish Parliament's Debating Chamber. Over the next 20 years, we want to be able to say we seized every opportunity to take big leaps forward on equality; we want a Parliament that reflects the society it represents and for that Parliament to take decisions which eradicate economic, social and political inequality. A Scotland which radically advances the lives of those who need it most. Only then will devolution have truly succeeded in making Scotland the very best it can be.

*Dear Scottish Parliament...*

I am not from Scotland and I have only lived here for two years, however I have noticed a few things. Poverty is a big thing all around the world including Scotland and I feel that over the next 20 years you can change that.

If you can help stop poverty this can help with a lot of other minor things too like littering. The more people on the street, the more things are left behind as the homeless move from one place to the other. If we can keep this country clean, we can do other things too. We can reduce the use of fossil fuels that make our country polluted.

Another point is education. Education is very important, it is what makes the young people of today (including me) independent and more and more people are not getting this education.

*Etieno Essien, 13, Aberdeen*

CHAPTER 11

# Some Questions on Sovereignty and Free Speech

### CHARLES ROBERT

TWENTY YEARS AGO, on 12 May 1999, the Scottish Parliament met for the first time. On that historic day, Dr Winnifred Ewing, as the oldest member, opened the sitting with the words 'The Scottish Parliament, which adjourned on 25 March 1707, is hereby reconvened'. This memorable statement spoke of a long-standing determination to have greater control in the management of local, domestic affairs, to establish 'home rule' for Scotland. The new Scottish Parliament, however, is not entirely like its historic predecessor. It is not a sovereign body established under the Crown of Scotland, but rather a devolved assembly with limited, defined powers created by statute enacted by the UK Parliament. The Scotland Act 1998 provides for a regional government based on the Westminster model. The act is like similar initiatives adopted at the same time which renewed regional government in Northern Ireland and allowed it for Wales. The Scotland Act authorises a government to administer certain domestic matters, raise revenues, legislate and be accountable to a unicameral parliament located in Edinburgh whose members are elected for a fixed term on the basis of mixed-member proportional representation.

The devolved status of the Scottish Parliament affects significant aspects of its character including the rights, immunities and powers it possesses to enforce its authority and protect itself and its members from undue interference. The limited nature of these rights, immunities and powers became known early on. During a debate on a Freedom of Information Bill just one month after the first sitting, Margaret Ewing, MSP and a daughter-in-law of Dr Winifred Ewing, asked whether

> members of this Parliament [have] the same rights of parliamentary privilege as members at Westminster.

By way of reply, the Deputy First Minister and Minister for Justice, Jim Wallace, said that he was uncertain about this. While he believed that

Members of the Scottish Parliament did have the same privileges as in Westminster, he suggested taking the advice of the Presiding Officer, Sir David Steel. The Presiding Officer agreed to circulate a note on parliamentary privilege noting at the time that it differed 'slightly' from that at Westminster. The extent of this difference became somewhat clearer when the Presiding Officer authorised the publication of a business bulletin issued 6 August 1999. This bulletin explains that the Scottish Parliament

> does not derive rights by reference to privileges which exist... at Westminster and there is no concept of 'parliamentary privilege' in relation to the Scottish Parliament or its members in the sense understood at Westminster.

As a devolved parliament, the protections and immunities possessed by the Scottish Parliament are only those conferred on it by the Scotland Act.

These provisions are intended to give parliament sufficient protection to enable it to properly conduct its business. This was the same position taken by the Secretary of State for Scotland and its future First Minister, Donald Dewar, during the second reading debate on the bill at Westminster. The bulletin describes the limited nature and scope of some of these protections. It concludes by acknowledging that this is a 'complex area of the law' which is expected to develop over time, and it is not to be regarded as a 'comprehensive statement'. Again, this echoed the views of Mr Dewar who recognised that ultimately it would be for the Scottish Parliament to decide how to conduct its business. The provisions of the act were 'a useful starting point'.

Twenty years on, it is perhaps time to review that 'starting point' and assess what developments have occurred in this 'complex area of the law'. The Scottish Parliament has matured and has become an integral element of Scottish public life. The scope of its responsibilities has increased and is likely to expand further in the future. With this history and growing mandate, it might be appropriate to consider whether certain limitations imposed by its devolved status should be adjusted. Its current rights and immunities might be strengthened to enable the Scottish Parliament to carry out its functions better. The Scotland Act should perhaps be amended to allow parliament greater autonomy, giving it more control over its internal procedures and deliberations. Beyond this, in any reassessment of these rights and powers, it might also be worthwhile to rethink their purpose, put in place practices that both protect the necessary functions of parliament and, at the same time, better safeguard the legitimate rights of citizens. While certain aspects of the current arrangement already provide for some of this, more could be done to align parliament's rights, immunities and powers with the expectations of a modern rights-based legal framework. These are important issues worth exploring as the Scottish Parliament celebrates its 20th anniversary.

As noted in the August 1999 business bulletin, among the provisions of the Scotland Act that protect parliament are those conferred through subsection 28(5) which prevent any challenge to the validity of its proceedings with respect to the consideration of a bill once it has become an act of the Scottish Parliament. Section 40 of the act limits the sort of remedy that can be sought against parliament, any member, the staff or the Presiding Officer, through the parliamentary corporate body which has responsibility for the management of property, staff and services required for parliament's purposes. Section 41 provides for immunity in relation to proceedings in parliament against defamation. Any statement made during 'proceedings of the Parliament' and the publication of any statement under the authority of the Parliament are absolutely privileged. As the bulletin then explains, this immunity is designed to protect parliament and its members so that they can publish and debate without fear of being threatened with defamation suits. While this protection is absolute with respect to defamation,

> it does not shield members from the operation of the law in relation to other matters, for example, incitement to racial hatred.

The bulletin also notes that proceedings of the Parliament can be subject to the law of contempt of court, a limitation not imposed on the deliberations of Westminster or its members. Article 9 of the Bill of Rights 1689 puts the proceedings beyond any scrutiny or control by the courts. In the Scottish Parliament, however:

> 'Rule 7.3.2 of the standing orders (Order in the Chamber) includes a requirement that members shall not conduct themselves in a manner which would constitute a contempt of court (or indeed would constitute a criminal offence)'.

According to the 'strict liability rule' established through the Contempt of Court Act 1981, conduct may be treated as a contempt of court if it is seen to interfere with the course of justice with respect to court proceedings regardless of any intent to do so. The liability to a contempt charge applies equally to publications where there is a substantial risk that it could impede or prejudice a case before the courts. There is an exception to this strict liability rule. Under Section 42 of the Scotland Act, publications of the proceedings of the Parliament made in relation to a bill or subordinate legislation or to fair and accurate reports of such proceedings made in good faith are exempt from the strict liability rule. The purpose of this exemption is to allow parliament to legislate without the risk of coming under the jurisdiction of the courts.

The freedom of debate applied to bills or subordinate legislation does not include debate that is subject to the rule of *sub judice*. Rule 7.5 (*sub judice*) prohibits a member from referring to any matter in relation to which legal proceedings are active except to the extent permitted by the Presiding Officer. Should a member refer to a legal proceeding that is deemed active, without the permission of the Presiding Officer or by exceeding the limits of that permission, the member can be ordered to stop. If the *sub judice* rule is breached, the member could face a suspension of his rights and privileges based on a review under the Code of Conduct as well as being subject to the strict liability rule. Indeed, even with the permission of the Presiding Officer, a member remains at risk of contempt of court if the member's remarks are not found to be as limited as they should be.

Deference to the courts that limits the protection of Members of the Scottish Parliament in debate also constrains the power of committees with respect to testimony of witnesses and production of papers. Section 23 of the Scotland Act deals with the authority of parliament to require the attendance of witnesses for giving evidence or producing documents 'concerning any subject for which any Member of the Scottish Executive has general responsibility'. According to Sections 25 and 26 of the Act, uncooperative witnesses are liable to various offences on summary conviction which can lead to imprisonment not exceeding three months or to a 'level five fine'. Included in these offences are failure to attend or to provide requested documents, tampering with testimony or documents, and refusal to take an oath when required to do so. At the same time, however, subsection 23(9) makes it clear that a person is not obliged to answer any question or produce any document which he would be entitled to refuse to answer or produce in a court in Scotland.

The failure of witnesses to co-operate before parliamentary committees either because they will not, or because they should not, is determined by the courts, not parliament. Unlike Westminster, there is no claim of exclusive cognisance that puts such issues under the sole control of the Scottish Parliament. In matters involving discipline, parliament has little authority; it is dependent on the courts and their interpretation of the provisions of the Scotland Act.

The relationship between parliament and the courts established through the Scotland Act is an innovative way to respect the distinct roles of these two branches of government. Each is expected to support the authority of the other. Each is meant to avoid undue interference in the operations of the other. For neither is it a question of asserting supremacy; rather it is one of maintaining mutual sovereignty. Debate in parliament is not to impede the work of the courts nor should parliament insist on seeking information that would exceed judicial standards or norms. For its part, the courts will support the legitimate authority of parliament by adjudicating cases of contempt and non-compliance with the orders of parliament, imposing penalties where appropriate.

Despite the balance between parliament and the courts struck under the Scotland Act, which is generally appropriate, there is one area of this mutually supportive relationship that is at risk. The devolved status of parliament and its dependence on the Scotland Act means that the courts through their power to interpret the law can intrude into the proper jurisdiction of parliament. Whether intentionally or not, this can undermine the right of parliament to govern its internal procedures and how it deals with legislation.

This risk was exposed in an early court case that challenged the right of a member to sponsor a hunting bill. In the Court of Session, several petitioners sought to prevent a member from introducing a bill because of allegations of receiving a benefit from supporters who wanted to ban certain forms of hunting. They argued that this was in violation of Article 6 of the Scotland Act forbidding a member from doing anything in any proceeding of Parliament which would benefit a person from whom the member has received or expects to receive a remuneration. The Lord

Ordinary, Lord Johnston, who decided the case at trial preferred to be flexible about the legal status of parliament. Even though he recognised that the Scottish Parliament was a creature of statute, he accepted that it had some autonomy over its proceedings and deliberations. As he put it:

> The Scottish Parliament is entitled to make its own determination... upon its own rules and this court should not even look at it on grounds of irrationality... What I am entirely satisfied about is that it is quite inappropriate for pressure groups, or individuals, however their interests may be affected, to have the right to tell, by way of legal action, a committee of this Parliament that its own view of its own rules is inappropriate or even wrong.

On appeal, the Inner House was unable to endorse the remarks of the Lord Ordinary on the relationship between the courts and the Scottish Parliament precisely because the Scottish Parliament as a product of statute law only possesses, and is limited to, those powers provided by law. More importantly, the exercise of those powers is susceptible to the authority of the courts that interpret that law. As to the view that the court might exercise a 'self-denying ordinance in relation to interfering with the proceedings' of parliament, The Lord President, Lord Rodger, rejected this approach. While the courts can

> be expected to accord all due respect to the Parliament as to any other litigant, they must equally be aware that they are not dealing with a parliament which is sovereign: on the contrary, it is subject to the law and hence to the courts.

The Lord President justified this position by explaining that applying the self-denying ordinance for the benefit of parliament could deny the legitimate rights of other parties under the law. For him,

> the correct attitude in such cases must be to apply the law in an even-handed way.

This judgement coming so soon after its establishment underscored a limit to the immunities and protection allowed the Scottish Parliament. It confirmed the proposition of the Presiding Officer's bulletin that the

Scottish Parliament has only the rights and powers explicitly granted under the Scotland Act. It has no right to claim any parliamentary privilege possessed and exercised by Westminster not expressly included in the Scotland Act. As a result, the Scottish Parliament does not have total control over its deliberations and is not the sole judge of the lawfulness of its own proceedings. Unlike Westminster, the rights and safeguards of the Scottish Parliament and its members do not exclude the jurisdiction of the courts. The Scottish Parliament does not have the authority to claim exclusive cognisance that would keep the courts from having a role in cases that challenge the procedures used to conduct its business. This is an issue that merits reconsideration.

One particular aspect of the judgment by the Lord President stands out. In looking at the situation in Scotland with its limited autonomy, he questioned the position of those who believed it was inconsistent with the very idea of parliament that it should be subject to the law of the land and the jurisdiction of the courts. He disagreed with this view and went further to state that, if anything,

> it is the Parliament of Westminster which is unusual in being respected as sovereign by the courts... By contrast, in many democracies throughout the Commonwealth, for example, even where the parliaments have been modelled in some respects on Westminster, they owe their existence and powers to statute and are in various ways subject to the law and to the courts which act to uphold the law.

In taking this position, that Westminster's immunity from intervention by the courts in its proceedings was the exception rather than the rule, the Lord President overstated the case. He appears to have overlooked the numerous judgments across the Commonwealth applying the principle first expressed in Bradlaugh v. Gossett (1884) that acknowledged parliamentary privilege and the right and necessity of parliaments to control their proceedings, their claim to exclusive cognisance, free from interference by the courts.

Indeed, the decision to limit the powers and immunities of the Scottish Parliament, as well as of the other devolved legislatures, was a significant departure from historical practice in dealing with colonial or sub-national parliaments dating back centuries. For many of the early legislatures established in the American colonies, the Caribbean, Canada, Australia and New Zealand, particularly prior to the recognition of a responsible government, claiming and exercising all the parliamentary privileges of Westminster was an essential objective. These colonial legislatures insisted on such privileges and in some cases were prepared to invoke them without the sanction of the home government and over the objections of the royal governor. Like the House of Commons itself in the 17th century, they realised that the absence of these privileges, including the protection of Article 9 of the Bill of Rights, would cripple any attempt on their part to effectively establish a role that could challenge the authority of an assertive governor acting on behalf of the Crown. In the end, Westminster relented and bowed to the inevitable.

As responsible government took hold across Britain's colonial empire, the laws enacting colonial constitutions often included a provision granting the privileges of the House of Commons to the new Parliament. This happened as early as the 1850s with the separate colonies of Australia, followed by New Zealand, Canada, and the Australian Commonwealth. This concession was also made when parliamentary government was established in Ireland through the Government of Ireland Acts of 1914 and 1920. The object of these latter acts was, finally, to provide for home rule through the creation of devolved parliaments and both contained provisions allowing these parliaments to claim the full range of privileges exercised by the House of Commons at Westminster. Subsection 18(1) of the Government of Ireland Act 1920, stated that:

> The powers, privileges and immunities of the Senate and House of Commons of Southern Ireland and the Senate and House of Commons of Northern Ireland, and of the members and of the committees thereof, shall be such as may be defined by Act of the Parliament in question, and, until so defined, shall be those held and enjoyed by the Commons House of Parliament of the United Kingdom and its members and committees at the date of the passing of this Act.

This act as it applied to Stormont, the Parliament of Northern Ireland, remained in force until replaced by the Northern Ireland Act 1998.

The current jurisdiction of the courts to supervise the legislative deliberations of the Scottish Parliament risks challenging its autonomy and undermining its authority. Though this has caused little harm to date, it is not a desirable situation, and as the Scottish Parliament celebrates its

20th anniversary, as it continues to mature and assume more responsibilities, it might be appropriate to consider further clarifying its proper independence from the courts with respect to its proceedings. The justification for having the courts involved in instances where witnesses are exposed to the possibility of sanctions is that it ensures due process and avoids undue partisanship. The ability of the courts to interfere in the deliberations of parliament or its committees oversteps the boundaries that should separate these two branches of government. To reduce and avoid any strain in their relations, the Scotland Act should be amended by Westminster to limit the role of the courts in their ability to inquire into proceedings in parliament. This would be a welcome change that would recognise the significant role that parliament has in providing effective government for Scotland.

Such an important adjustment to the relationship between parliament and the courts would reinforce its overall innovative and balanced character. It would build on and strengthen the mutual respect and support that is intended to govern their interactions. In the history of the relations between these two branches of government across the Commonwealth, this relationship remains exceptional, but it should be encouraged.

In the 21st century, the freedom of debate guaranteed to parliament and its members that is protected by the courts should not be the cause of unnecessary harm to citizens. The dignity and authority of parliament are not enhanced when free speech attacks or damages the name or reputation of a citizen with impunity. Members no longer deserve to be completely protected when committing defamation. This is a matter that deserves the attention of the Scottish Parliament and, because of its recent creation, it seems better placed to deal with the problem than other, more established, Parliaments. As is clearly shown by Australia and New Zealand as well as Westminster, the older Parliaments remain caught up in their history and have had only limited success in dealing with the challenge even though they have acknowledged the risk.

The guarantee of free speech was needed originally to protect parliament not from the people, but from the King and the courts he controlled. The historic rivalry between parliament and the Crown escalated over the 17th century and led to the English Civil War. The eventual outcome, following the Restoration and the accession of William and Mary, favoured parliament and led to the explicit recognition of free speech as an undoubted privilege in the Bill of Rights. Absolute free speech was claimed as necessary by all parliaments established throughout the Empire and Commonwealth including the Scottish Parliament to the end of the 20th century. Unfettered free speech is seen as an indispensable right and immunity. Yet this model, this paradigm, must now shift to accommodate a legal reality that has emerged over the second half of the last century, one that admits to a paramount rights-based culture. This shift requires parliament to exercise free speech in a more responsible way, one that is more deliberately accountable.

The risk of free speech abuse, of defamation, inadvertent or not, is real and potentially substantial. This risk has become greater and more damaging as the debates of parliament are transmitted by other means in addition to the traditional printed Hansard. For decades now, many parliaments, like Scotland's, have televised their proceedings to reach their citizens, to demonstrate their relevance and to prove their accountability. Access to parliamentary deliberations has also been expanded to include social media that continues its penetration into every corner of the public sphere. Limited attempts to mitigate the risk of free speech abuse testify to its reality but these have not really kept up with dynamics of modern technology. Since 1997 the Australian House of Representatives has used a Citizen's Right of Reply to answer parliamentary statements that have adversely affected their name or reputation or unreasonably invaded their privacy. The procedure involves the submission of a complaint to the Speaker with an appropriate response from the citizen to be incorporated into the parliamentary record as an appendix to Hansard. If the Speaker finds the complaint valid, it is then submitted to the Committee of Privileges and Members' Interests. If the committee also agrees that the complaint has merit, its decision must be reported to the House. If the House adopts the recommendation of the committee, the response will be printed in Hansard. This complex, time consuming, paper-based procedure does little to address effectively the harm done by free speech abuse. It is hardly proportionate to the potential damage to name and reputation. Better alternatives deserve to be considered.

Perhaps the best way to limit the damage of free speech abuse is to make members directly responsible for its prevention. This is what Germany has done. The first article of its Constitution states as a fundamental principle that human dignity shall be inviolable. To respect and protect it shall be the duty of all state authority.

The consequences of this declaration are evident in the section dealing with members' immunities. Section 46.1 states that a member cannot be

subjected to court proceedings or disciplinary action or otherwise called to account outside the Bundestag for a vote cast or for any speech or debate in the Bundestag or in any of its committees.

However, this immunity does not include defamation. In unambiguous terms, 'This provision shall not apply to defamatory insults'. Any charge of defamation will be resolved through the courts. In the 70 years that the constitution has been in force, no charge has ever been laid. The simple lesson seems to be that exposure to the liability of defamation has encouraged members to be prudent in debate.

The Scottish Parliament has already provided that any incitement to hatred in debate will not be protected by the free speech privilege of members. Out of respect for its citizens, it does not seem much of a stretch to insist that members be held liable to prosecution in the courts if they commit defamation. Making an amendment to the Scotland Act like the provision of the German Constitution would be an effective way to reduce the likelihood of defamation and, should it occur, provide a meaningful way to deal with it.

In the alternative, it is possible to put in place a procedure to deal with accusations of defamation internally. Under such a scheme, the privilege of free speech under the Scotland Act would remain in force, but it might require an amendment to the act to ensure the validity of the procedure and grant parliament the authority to examine a defamation complaint as a breach of the Members' Code of Conduct. The purpose of the amendment would forestall a likely challenge to the courts. As an internal matter, a charge of defamation could be assessed by the Presiding Officer or an appropriate neutral official designated by parliament. Upon completion of an investigation, the finding plus a recommendation for any sanction could be referred to the Code of Conduct Committee. In addition to requiring the member to make a full apology in the House, the committee could propose that the member be suspended for a period of time and pay a fine commensurate with what the law currently allows.

Again, based on the experience of the German model, the purpose of such a proposal would be to avoid defamation. If members are aware that they are not protected, they will more likely take steps to avoid exposing themselves to any corrective action. After all, the interests of citizens and the protection of their rights are better maintained by respecting them rather than having to resort to measures to punish those who trespass them.

On the first day of its sitting, Dr Ewing claimed kinship between the Scottish Parliament and its ancient predecessor. In fact, the new Parliament is much better. It is a modern legislative assembly holding accountable the Scottish Government in the tradition of the Westminster model. It possesses limited rights, immunities and powers that are better scaled to the expectations of the times. As a devolved Parliament, it has a well-balanced, co-ordinated relationship with the courts based on shared respect for the rule of law supporting a rights-based legal culture. While adjustments should be made between the courts and parliament to reduce the risk of interference in the proper conduct of its proceedings, the overall relationship still deserves to be considered a template for other jurisdictions. Similarly, the Scottish Parliament is better placed than most to finally abandon defamation as a protected right of free speech. Defamation has no legitimate role in the conduct of parliament and the debates of its members; it is an affront to the core purpose of parliament to represent and defend the rights and interests of citizens. It undermines the dignity and authority of parliament that is the justification for these protected rights. Whether or not these issues are addressed, it does little to diminish the pride that should be felt as the Scottish Parliament celebrates its 20th anniversary. From its beginning, the Parliament has assumed a place in the civic life of Scotland that has confirmed the value of home rule by providing effective government based on solid democratic values.

[The views expressed in this chapter are those of the author alone and do not necessarily reflect those of the House of Commons of Canada.]

*Dear Scottish Parliament...*

What a journey you have had. 20 years ago, the Scottish people were granted a voice. 20 years ago, we were given the power to change our country.

The power that the Parliament gives the Scottish people is amazing. We get our say on our devolved powers and so much more.

The Scottish Parliament has, for me, opened so many pathways with their focus on education.

The Scottish Parliament was ground-breaking in 1999, and it still is 20 years later in 2019.

Scotland still has a long way to go, but it is great to know that it is in safe hands with our MSPs; I hope to be one of these building blocks in the future, helping to make Scotland a better place.

In 20 years, I hope that I will be sitting in that Parliament as an MSP, and my big dream is to become the First Minister of Scotland. This is a big dream of mine because I would like to make some amazing changes in our world. Another big reason that I would like to be the first gay First Minister. It would mean a lot to both myself and the LGBT+ community. I would like to show children that are growing up in 20 years that it is okay to be LGBT+, and not only that but you can be a change-maker too. You can make an impact on the world.

Thank you, Scottish Parliament, for building a better and more united Scotland. I can only wish that your legacy continues for generations to come. It only takes one person to stand up and make a change and the rest will follow.

Thank you.

*Ewan Carmichael, 13, East Ayrshire*

CHAPTER 12

# A New Voice in the Land

JIM WALLACE

1 JULY 1999 is a day well etched in my memory. A host of images flood back – the procession, with my children, to the new Parliament from the old one; the final verse of 'A Man's a Man for A' That', when those in the Chamber joined in; some amazing sky acrobatics in Princes Street; the eloquence of the speech by the First Minister Donald Dewar:

> 'There shall be a Scottish Parliament'. Through long years, those words were first a hope, then a belief, then a promise. Now they are a reality... today there is a new voice in the land, the voice of a democratic Parliament. A voice to shape Scotland, a voice for the future.

Now, 20 years on, it's time to reflect on how that voice has shaped Scotland – and how it will be a voice to shape the future.

## What Were the Early Achievements?

Essentially the transition to devolved government was a smooth one. Given the wide range of responsibilities devolved to the Parliament and Executive on 1 July 1999 – the NHS, education, universities and colleges, the legal system, the criminal justice system, industrial promotion, internal transport, local government, tourism, culture, planning, housing, farming, fishing – all these activities and services continued to function under a Scottish Parliament without the skies falling in.

But that was a reflection on a well-established administration. There was more to the success than not falling down on the job.

Major policy and political issues such as the abolition of university tuition fees, and the introduction of free personal care for the elderly enjoyed obvious prominence. However, some less high-profile issues illustrate how the voice of a democratic parliament helped to shape Scotland.

I recall being lobbied at Westminster about implementation of the Scottish Law Commission's proposals on improving the legal arrangements for adults with incapacity. Westminster never found time for this legislation, but it was one of the first pieces of substantive legislation to pass through the Scottish Parliament. An Orkney solicitor later remarked to me that he had had cause to look out an old file and had forgotten how archaic the old procedures were in comparison to what we put in its place.

The new Parliament abolished feudal land tenure, updated the law relating to the very Scottish institution of the tenement, modernised procedures in the High Court, and introduced a victims' charter. We set ambitious targets for renewable energy. We passed more liberal and effective Freedom of Information legislation than Westminster. We led the way within the UK, in promoting a smoking ban in public places.

One of the searing memories of my early days as Justice Minister was when, on 2 August 1999, the Sheriff at Lanark directed the absolute discharge of Mr Noel Ruddle from the State Hospital at Carstairs. Mr Ruddle had been committed to the hospital, having pled guilty to contraventions of the Firearms Act – a Kalashnikov rifle – and to culpable homicide. The Sheriff concluded that Ruddle was no longer suffering from such a mental disorder which made it appropriate for him to continue to be detained in hospital for medical treatment. Furore ensued, and within weeks of the decision, the Parliament passed its first piece of legislation – the Mental Health Public Safety and Appeals (Scotland) Act 1999. It is questionable whether Westminster would have acted so quickly to block this legal loophole.

The act was subsequently challenged by some patients in the State Hospital, but in dismissing the case, the Judicial Committee of the Privy Council said:

The Scottish Ministers who took office in May 1999 were quick to appreciate the shortcoming of the existing legislation and although the new Scottish Parliament was only formally established on 1 July 1999 steps were taken with remarkable expedition to secure that some legislation was in place at an early date to guard against what was seen as a potential risk of danger to members of the public.

I remember reflecting, ruefully, that that judicial pronouncement didn't receive the same press coverage as the original lurid headlines.

## What Were the Trials and Tribulations?

Arguably those of us who campaigned for the Parliament could be accused of having oversold the new dawn which the new Parliament would herald. Few, if any of us ever claimed it was a shortcut to Nirvana, but there was an expectation that somehow all previous ills would disappear. And in some respects, we were seen to set off on the wrong foot. Awarding medals wasn't a smart move, even if MSPs themselves had little say in the matter. In the initial six-week period, before the Parliament acquired full powers, it was not possible to legislate, but some necessary housekeeping had to be done, such as fixing salaries and allowances. Inevitably this attracted allegations of self-serving MSPs, conveniently ignoring the fact that staff couldn't be paid until the allowances order was passed. The Holyrood building project was something of an albatross around the neck of the first parliamentary term, even although MSPs hadn't been responsible for the original letting of the contract and its terms.

I certainly counted myself among those who wanted a parliament which didn't simply transplant the culture and procedures of the Parliament by the Thames to the Mound and later to Holyrood. Did we succeed? To a considerable extent we did. The voting system was always likely to produce no overall majority for any one party. (The fact that it did in 2011, is possibly as much an aberration as the first-past-the-post system failing to produce a majority government in 2010 and 2017.) There was an expectation that there would be a coalition after 1999, or at least that the voting system would produce greater inter-party co-operation. I'm biased, but I do think that the coalition government from 1999 to 2007 ensured that the Parliament was established on a firm foundation. If anything, the criticism by 2007 was that it had become predictable and boring. Possibly this was a consequence of a seeking consensus and a culture of consultation. Whilst a coalition agreement ensured the buy-in of the coalition parties and the election – twice – of new First Ministers, we probably should have considered ways of refreshing the programme mid-term.

One source of political rough and tumble has been the replication of Prime Minister's Questions. FMQs is what the media focuses on. And having been on the receiving end on at least 15 occasions, I can testify that at times, it can certainly be lively. But too often, exchanges in the bear pit obscure the solid work, often achieved through consensus, in other areas of the Parliament's work.

## Committees

At the Parliament's outset, the committee system was seen as being a way in which we could differentiate ourselves from Westminster in a positive way. In a parliament where every party was a minority party, the committees, in theory at least, could be powerful bodies, holding the Executive to account. And by giving committees both a legislative scrutiny and an investigative role, it was thought that a sense of collegiality among members would enhance their effectiveness and authority. Arguably, at first, it worked. In these early days, I considered the Scottish Parliament's committee system to be a marked improvement on what I had experienced in the House of Commons.

The Scottish Parliament committee, looking at a bill, examines the issue at Stage One before embarking on clause by clause scrutiny and amendment. The minister is not a member of the committee (nor is there a Whip present). The minister appears before the committee, argues for the clauses or the executive amendments, and explains the Executive's response to amendments tabled by committee members, or indeed other MSPs. In my experience, all committee members engaged in the process, and whilst the Executive succeeded often, nothing could be taken for granted. Very often a backbench amendment would only be withdrawn on undertakings of further consideration and discussion with the member.

That was a considerable contrast with Westminster, as I had known it. MPs on committees examining bills were more likely to be doing constituency correspondence (especially on the government side) than participating. There was a ministerial reluctance to entertain anything from the opposition or backbench. And the membership of a minister and Whip on the committee secured a discipline, which not always manifested itself on the Mound or, later, at Holyrood.

On several occasions, I was on the receiving end of committee members asserting their independence from the Executive. In 2000, the Cabinet voted against the inclusion of a religion question in the 2001 census, and I had a very difficult time trying to justify the decision before the Equal Opportunities Committee. Indeed, so unpersuasive was I, that

I had to bring in the legislation to meet the committee's will. In a similar vein, I had to bow to the inevitable and water-down proposals for a smacking ban and for raising the age of criminal responsibility in Scotland; issues which have resurfaced in recent months.

I took the view that such reversals showed the genuine spirit of committee engagement, which I had hoped for. Admittedly, today, I view from a distance; but I have heard sufficient reports to suggest that in the Parliament's second decade such a spirit of committee independence has not been as robust. Going forward, the committees will hopefully be robust in their scrutiny of the Executive's actions and legislation.

In the meantime, Westminster may claim to have learned some lessons (consciously or otherwise) from Holyrood. Public Bill Committees now hear evidence before detailed consideration of a bill and select committees have shown a much greater readiness to criticise the Government than in the past. Now is surely the time for Holyrood committees to rediscover a greater independence, as well as learn other lessons from Westminster, such as the election of committee chairs (which would continue to be allocated on a party basis) by secret ballot of all MSPs.

And although it is rarely popular to raise the issue of payment to politicians, I do think Holyrood should examine the Commons experience of paying committee chairs a salary. Done properly, it is an onerous task beyond the mainstream duties of an MSP. It may also reflect the stature to which committees ought to aspire.

One criticism of the Holyrood committee system is that the combined roles of legislative scrutiny and investigative inquiry is too burdensome, and the pressure of legislation can mean that inquiries must take a back seat. It is certainly true that in the early days of the Parliament, the Justice Committee had to be split in two because of the volume of justice related legislation. That undoubtedly curbed the time available for investigative inquiries.

The criticism shouldn't detract from some worthwhile inquiries undertaken by committees over the last 20 years (including important post-legislative scrutiny). Nevertheless, it is a criticism which ought to be considered. The simple fact is that with 129 MSPs, a proportion of whom are ministers or office-holders, it is difficult to see how there could be a division of committee responsibilities without imposing an intolerable burden on members or making committees so small that they lack critical mass for proper effectiveness.

Moreover, following the Scotland Acts of 2012 and 2016, the Scottish Parliament now has much greater responsibilities, not least in relation to taxation and social security. If ministers are to be scrutinised properly in their exercise of these powers, we surely cannot afford an over-stretched committee system. I believe there is now a case for increasing the number of MSPs. Although the Constitutional Convention reached agreement in principle on the electoral system, there was impasse between the Scottish Labour Party and Scottish Liberal Democrats over the size of the Parliament. Labour wanted 113 members and the Lib Dems wanted 145, not least to secure greater proportionality. George Robertson and I met and agreed to split the difference! Adding two additional members to the eight electoral regions would achieve an increase without a major boundary redistribution – and would secure greater proportionality.

## Future Relationships

Speaking with Donald Dewar in the early days of the Scottish Government, we reflected how important personal relationships (both at ministerial and official level) were in making a success of devolution, and how much more difficult that would become, as time passed, and paths diverged.

In the first Cabinet, Donald Dewar, Sam Galbraith, Henry McLeish and Andrew Hardie had all served in UK Government, and I had been a Member of the House of Commons for 16 years. The personal relationships were invaluable in oiling the relationships between the two administrations.

As ministers, we were encouraged by the First Minister to establish contacts with our Westminster counterparts and to deal directly with them, bypassing the Scotland Office. The Secretary of State and the Scotland Office were viewed as a sort of seventh cavalry, to be turned to as a last resort.

Scottish Parliament committees and select committees of Lords and Commons have produced insightful reports on the relationships between the UK Parliament and Government and the devolved legislatures and administrations. I chaired a small sub-group of the Calman Commission in 2008–09, which looked at the issue – and whose recommendations still, in my view, are pertinent today. With Brexit and the likelihood of UK frameworks substituting for EU frameworks in some key areas, these links are even more crucial.

The Joint Ministerial Committees (JMCs), which have operated from the outset have been classic cases of the curate's egg. Looking to improve the inter-governmental arrangements, it would be helpful to put JMCs on a more formal footing with a secretariat, schedule of meetings, agendas agreed by the secretariat with the respective administrations, much greater transparency and a recognition by the UK Government that there will be occasions when it has a potential conflict of interest between 'holding the ring' as the UK Government and a specific interest as the department with responsibility for the issue in England. On these occasions, it would be better for a Secretary of State to chair a meeting and a junior minister from the department to represent the English interest. I don't pretend that that is a total panacea. Personal relationships still matter, even if lack of familiarity makes them more difficult to forge.

Another positive change would be in culture. Too often, it seems, meetings have been the forum for addressing disputes or airing grievances (accompanied by the appropriate press release). It would be an improvement if some meetings could have a more positive agenda: exploring issues of common concern and trying to identify joint solutions, or, indeed, looking to where the lessons can be learned from the experience of other administrations.

My fear in moving forward is that, in a very British constitutional way, we shall have a series of *ad hoc* arrangements in different spheres of activity where common UK frameworks are required but these will lack consistency and coherence. We need an overarching framework, with similar structures for discussion and decision-making. The Welsh Government published a paper, 'Brexit and Devolution' in June 2017, which contains some far-reaching proposals as to how UK frameworks might operate, including the establishment of a UK Council of Ministers and something akin to 'qualified majority voting'. I suspect that the proposals are too radical for the present UK Government to contemplate, but imaginative thinking is required to avoid impasses.

But it's not only future relationships between Holyrood and Westminster which require attention. From the Parliament's outset, Scottish ministers have engaged in promoting Scotland abroad and forging links with other sub-member state governments, as well as supporting international development initiatives. In a post-Brexit world, these links and initiatives should be fostered. In trade negotiations, there will inevitably be competence overlaps, where the reserved power to make international treaties coincides with the devolved subject-matter of the treaties. It is essential that clear understandings and *modus operandi* are established to allow for the full engagement of Scottish ministers on issues where there is a devolved responsibility. It would be worth looking at international examples, such as in Canada, where some effort has been made to address the issue of concurrent responsibilities.

Nor should we be afraid to examine how the devolution settlement may be adapted and extended to enable Scottish ministers, on appropriate occasions, to enter into binding international agreements. It sounds radical, but Flanders has had several international competences since 1993, in accordance with the principle *'in foro interno, in foro externo'* – each minister has the power to decide on European and international initiatives within their own responsibilities. So, for example, if the UK fails to reach agreement with the EU on studentships or research funding, isn't there a case for Scotland being able to negotiate its own arrangement, to the extent that these issues are devolved?

Closer to home, a third key relationship is with local government. I always feared that the arrival of the Parliament could pose a challenge to the standing of local government. Prior to the Parliament's creation, politicians on all sides talked – and I believe genuinely – about 'parity of esteem'. On 2 July 1999, the day after the Parliament was opened, the report by Neil McIntosh, commissioned by the Labour Government to examine the Parliament and local government was published. That report, in turn, paved the way for the Kerley Committee and thus for PR for local government. Making local councils more representative of the people they serve is arguable the most significant development in relation to local government since 1999.

But notwithstanding initiatives at the outset to reduce ring-fencing and establish a power of local initiative, predictable tensions have emerged. The Constitutional Convention, whose final report is peppered with references to the European Charter of Local Self-Government, concluded that in any future review of local government

> the aim of the Parliament should be, firstly, to safeguard and where possible increase the area of discretion available at the level of the local authority.

The story of the second decade of the Scottish Parliament, however, has been one of increasing centralisation. Only now is local taxation ceasing to be dictated by central government. Police and fire services have been centralised in a way which hasn't exactly covered the idea in glory. Local courts have been closed. Local government funding has been squeezed further than overall Holyrood expenditure, thus limiting the scope for local initiative. As someone who believes in decentralised decision-making, this is very troubling.

Regrettably, the issue of local government reform always seems to raise the spectre of boundary changes and altering the number of councils. There may be limited scope for rationalising council boundaries, to enhance cross-boundary co-operation in the provision of certain services, or to establish, where there is demand, new burgh councils in some of the larger rural council areas, and to devolve appropriate powers to them. However, a thorough-going reform of local government should look at reforms of council finances, both about the mode of local taxation and devising a way whereby local government can be less reliant on central government for its funding.

These are just some suggestions as to how a new balance between the Scottish Parliament and local government and local communities can be struck. Parliament, in partnership with local government, should have the confidence and vision to ensure that the spirit of local government and local determination is revitalised. The extent to which parliament can rise to the challenge of reforming local government finance and revitalising local democracy should be a measure of its success in its third decade.

## Conclusion

In all my years of campaigning for a Scottish Parliament, I was adamant that its creation wasn't a goal in itself. The most liberating election campaign which I ever fought was the first election to the Scottish Parliament in 1999. To a greater or lesser extent, all the general elections in which I'd been a candidate, had been fought against a backdrop of an ongoing constitutional debate about Scotland's future. By 1999, we had a Parliament, endorsed overwhelmingly in the 1997 referendum; so now we could debate what the Parliament was going to do.

Is it too much to hope for that in the first election of the Parliament's third decade, the issues of health, education, transport, local government, the environment and, reflecting the new powers, tax and social security will be to the fore? In his speech at the opening of the Parliament on 1 July 1999, Donald Dewar also said:

> We are fallible. We will make mistakes. But we will never lose sight of what brought us here: the striving to do right by the people of Scotland; to respect their priorities; to better their lot; and to contribute to the commonweal.

Yes, mistakes are made, they are at least our mistakes, and we should shake off the knee-jerk response always to blame Westminster. But compared to many countries with devolved powers, the competences of the Scottish Parliament and the Scottish ministers are extensive – more extensive today than they were in 1999. So, let our Parliamentarians resolve again to use them – to better the lot of the people of Scotland, and contribute to the common weal.

*Dear Scottish Parliament...*

I am not sure if the Scottish Parliament is well placed to tackle the big issues facing Scotland over the next 20 years.

The big issue is climate change. As a result of this we are getting more extreme weather.

I think the Scottish Parliament should listen to young people's views more and make political information easier to understand. My hopes are that the Scottish Parliament will prioritise tackling global warming which is a result of climate change. I feel very strongly about this as I am interested in geography.

I wish politicians were less intimidating. Young adults should be listened to as they are the future. There should be less discrimination as it can be really damaging to the victim's self-confidence.

I believe the Scottish Parliament should explain what all the political jargon means so people don't feel confused. There should also be information available in braille if you are blind and sign language if you are deaf or have a hearing impairment. This will make it more accessible for people.

My aspirations are for the politicians to help people with benefits. This will make it easier for them to apply without feeling stigmatised.

I hope people will be more respectful to people with learning difficulties.

Young people should be informed about any decisions made that affects their future. This will make them more aware of the decisions they can make and how to make them. Teenagers should be able to have a say in their life.

In conclusion I think the Scottish Parliament is doing a really good job.

*Hope Teal, 18, Perth and Kinross*

CHAPTER 13

# The Role of Law

CHRISTINE O'NEILL

SOMETIME IN 2000, at a conference organised by the Law Society of Scotland whose theme was nascent Scottish devolution, I participated in a workshop session led by Michael Clancy, then (and now) the society's Director of Law Reform. He will not remember it – I was a very newly qualified solicitor, and this was some years before I got to know Michael – but I clearly recall my question to him and his reply.

Given the complexities of the Scotland Act 1998 and the difficult questions that were bound to arise about the Parliament's powers, I asked, did he think it might be desirable for most, if not all, MSPs to be trained lawyers?

The question was clumsy and I (rightly) got a flea in my ear. I will have sounded naive and elitist – and ignorant of the numerous examples in Scottish and British history of political leaders who would be described in modern parlance as having little 'formal' education but who made profound contributions as parliamentarians. I hope I was none of those things. Instead I was, unsuccessfully, trying to make a more subtle point. Twenty years on, a further attempt.

Does an MSP, working in a parliament whose powers are prescribed in detail by statute, have a qualitatively different experience as a legislator than, say, an MP at Westminster whose powers are much less constrained? Do MSPs need to know more law, especially the law that governs the Parliament itself? Do concerns about the lawfulness of their activities trouble MSPs more than their counterparts in London?

I have not asked these questions of current and former MSPs and so cannot report the results of any empirical research. Others have investigated similar questions and the work of Dr Chris McCorkindale and Professor Janet Hiebert, of Strathclyde Law School and Queen's University Belfast respectively, is a valuable resource in understanding how the limits on the Parliament's powers affect participants in the law making process – government and parliamentary lawyers, Law Officers, the

Presiding Officer and MSPs – when they are preparing, introducing and debating proposed legislation. However, even their research involved interviewing a relatively small number of parliamentarians from the cohort in office in September 2015. There is no comprehensive picture of how (if at all) the legal framework governing the Parliament's work affects how MPs think of themselves or how they discharge their duties, and the extent to which that framework leads them to behave differently from MPs.

The distinctions between Holyrood's (and indeed the Welsh and Northern Ireland Assemblies') and Westminster's limits on legislative power should not be overstated. While the Supreme Court, in Gina Miller's challenge to the decision to give notice under Article 50 of the Treaty on European Union, reaffirmed sovereignty of the UK Parliament as 'the fundamental principle' of the British constitution there are, nevertheless, real constraints on what that Parliament can do. The most obvious is the requirement that, for as long as the UK remains a member of the European Union, Westminster legislation must not breach EU law. There is also the range of mechanisms created by the Human Rights Act 1998 intended to ensure that British laws, including Acts of Parliament, comply with the demands of the European Convention on Human Rights. While the British courts will not entertain challenges to the validity of Acts of Parliament on the grounds that they may not comply with the UK's (non-EU) international obligations, they will in many cases seek to interpret that legislation consistently complies with international law.

Nevertheless, the devolved legislatures are 'different'. As stated explicitly in Section 28 of the Scotland Act and as affirmed by the Supreme Court in 'Miller' (and despite the Sewel Convention) Westminster can legislate for Scotland in any subject area, including those that are devolved. By contrast, not only must the Scottish Parliament comply with EU law and with a range of rights conferred by the European Convention on Human Rights, but it must make law only for Scotland; its legislation must not 'relate to' the long list of reserved matters set out in Schedule 5 to the Scotland Act; and it must not breach the restrictions set out in Schedule 4 to the 1998 Act.

Schedule 4 contains a cornucopia of technical provisions. First, it sets out a list of (mostly) pre-devolution laws that Holyrood is forbidden from modifying at all, even where their subject matter would be thought to be devolved. The list includes some measures that are of obvious constitutional importance (including certain sections of the Articles of Union and the whole of the Human Rights Act 1998) as well as some that are altogether more mundane (for example parts of the Local Government, Planning and Land Act 1980 relating to the designation of enterprise zones). Second, Schedule 4 also lists the parts of the Scotland Act 1998 itself that the Scottish Parliament may not alter. Third it sets out complex rules on understanding what is meant by the law relating to reserved matters – an exercise that involves much more than simply reading the list of reservations in Schedule 5 (discussed below). The attempt by the Supreme Court in 2010 to explain those rules in a case was regarded as so unsatisfactory by the late Lord Rodger of Earlsferry (then sitting as a Justice of the Supreme Court and formerly Lord President of the Court of Session) that he described the majority's analysis as creating a 'new and intriguing mystery'. And, as we will come to, Schedule 4 also now prohibits the Scottish Parliament from modifying (most of) the European Union (Withdrawal) Act 2018.

While this scheme of devolution was never simple, I think it can be fairly argued that over the course of the last 20 years the task of understanding the boundaries of the Parliament's law-making powers has become progressively more difficult. Recent reforms and anticipated developments, particularly related to Brexit, will only add to the complexity. Looking forward to the next 20 years – assuming devolution continues as the foundation of the constitutional relationship between Scotland and the rest of the UK – it seems inevitable that questions about whether bills are within the Parliament's legislative competence (or whether executive action is within the powers of the Scottish Government) will become harder to answer. Two examples might illustrate the point.

The first 'new' complexity arises from the way in which more recent changes have been made to Schedule 5 to the Scotland Act, the part of the act which lists those areas reserved to Westminster. The 'reserved powers' model that was adopted for the Scotland Act 1998 – the basic premise of which is that the Scottish Parliament has 'plenary' power and can legislate in all areas except those subject to specific limits – was intended to bring greater clarity as to the Parliament's powers than would have been achieved from a 'transferring' model where the devolved legislature is given power only over a specific list of matters. A transferring model had been used for the Scotland Act 1978 and the 1998 act was a deliberate move away from that scheme. For various reasons the transferring model was used for Welsh devolution in 1998 but after a lengthy campaign, and by virtue of the Wales Acts 2014 and 2017, Wales now also enjoys a reserved powers model.

In the years since devolution there have been regular changes to the boundary between reserved and devolved powers. The vast majority of those changes have involved the transfer of additional powers to Holyrood, achieved by removing areas of law from the list of reserved matters or by keeping the reservation but creating new 'exceptions'. Algebraically, this may be expressed as:

*Legislative competence = power to legislate for everything - (reservations - exceptions to reservations)*

In many cases the changes were made with (relatively) little fanfare and by orders made by the UK Government – as was done, for example, between 2000 and 2004 when a range of railway powers were devolved to Scotland. In other cases amendments have been made by 'set piece' legislation such as the Scotland Act 2012 which implemented many of the recommendations of the Calman Commission's report of 2010 and carved out new 'exceptions' to reservations in areas including devolved taxes and firearms and which (in a surprise move) also reserved for the first time the regulation of activities in Antarctica. Reservations tend to be expressed as concerning a whole subject area, for example 'Control of nuclear, biological and chemical weapons and other weapons of mass destruction' or by reference to an existing statute, for example:

The subject-matter of Sections 16 and 16A of the National Heritage Act 1980 (public indemnities for objects on loan to museums, art galleries, etc).

There has always been room for argument about the precise meaning of a reservation. In anticipation of those arguments, the drafters of the bill that became the Scotland Act 1998 gave guidance to legislators and to the courts on how reservations should be interpreted. So, for example, Section 29(3) of the 1998 Act provides that

the question whether a provision of an Act of the Scottish Parliament relates to a reserved matter is to be determined... by reference to the purpose of the provision, having regard (among other things) to its effect in all the circumstances.

While early legal challenges to Acts of the Scottish Parliament focused not on the devolved/reserved boundary but on human rights issues, as the Parliament's legislative activity increased so did the range of questions asked of the courts by those affected by new laws.

So, for example, in its challenge to the Tobacco and Primary Medical Services (Scotland) Act 2010, Imperial Tobacco argued that the bans on the display of tobacco and on the use of tobacco vending machines introduced by the 2010 act related to the sale and supply of goods to consumers and to product safety: both reserved matters. The Supreme Court concluded that the *purposes* of the display and vending machine bans were to empower ministers to take action to make tobacco products less visible to potential consumers, thereby reducing sales, and to make cigarettes less readily available, particularly to children and young people, with a view to reducing smoking.

However, even where arguments arose about the precise content or meaning of a reservation, the terms of the reservation itself was relatively clear from the face of the Scotland Act.

That cannot be said with the same level of confidence about some of the reservations that were amended by the Scotland Act 2016, particularly that relating to social security. The Smith Commission, established in the wake of the 2014 independence referendum, recommended the devolution of the responsibility for a range of social security benefits, including powers to create new benefits in areas of devolved responsibility and to make discretionary payments in any area of welfare. These recommendations were given effect principally by amendments to Reservation F1 in Schedule 5 to the Scotland Act 1998. This reservation is now highly complex. It retains as a general reservation to Westminster

> schemes supported from central or local funds which provide assistance for social security purposes to or in respect of individuals by way of benefits

but now includes ten separate 'exceptions' to the general reservation. Some of those exceptions – which define the scope of devolved power in these areas – are drafted by reference to types of benefits such as disability benefits and carers' benefits. Others refer to specific legislation, such as the Social Work (Scotland) Act 1968, the Chronically Sick and Disabled Persons Act 1970 and the Children (Scotland) Act 1995. Yet others refer to the purpose for which a benefit might be made available, for example for meeting or reducing maternity or funeral expenses. The exceptions themselves are limited by a range of exclusions and Holyrood does not have power in relation 'reserved benefits'. Reservation F1 looks and feels like a 'transferred powers' provision grafted on to the reserved powers model.

This is not a complaint about complexity *per se*. The sharing of power over social security provision between the UK and devolved administrations is politically controversial and practically difficult to achieve. Implementation of the new powers has required primary legislation by the Scottish Parliament and the creation of Social Security Scotland. The complexity of the benefits system and of implementing devolution of payments has been acknowledged by Audit Scotland, most recently in its May 2018 report 'Social security: Implementing the devolved powers'. As devolution deepens into areas that might be regarded as 'core' responsibilities of the state, involving expenditure of very substantial public funds, it is perhaps inevitable that tensions over just how far devolution should go will be reflected in the legislative scheme. Rather the point is one about the (lack) of clarity of the law and its potential (in)accessibility to our parliamentarians – as well as those advising them and advising those affected by what they do.

The second bundle of new complexities comprises of those flowing from Brexit. Here, a very strong foretaste of the potential for future difficulty was given by the passage of and subsequent challenge to Holyrood's UK Withdrawal from the European Union (Legal Continuity) (Scotland) Bill, the lawfulness of which was disputed from the moment of its introduction. The bill was a response by the Scottish Parliament to the prospect of the UK's withdrawal from the European Union and, in particular, to the UK bill that eventually became the European Union (Withdrawal) Act 2018.

The overarching purpose of the UK bill was legal continuity: to ensure that, so far as possible, EU law remains in force within the UK immediately after Brexit. However, it also contained provisions affecting the devolution settlement (discussed below) that were opposed by the Scottish Government and Scottish Parliament, leading the latter to refuse consent to the bill in May 2018. Similar opposition came from the Welsh Assembly and Welsh Government.

The Scottish bill represented the Scottish Parliament's own approach to continuity. Many of its provisions mirrored those included in the Westminster bill but with significant differences. Some of those reflected an ambition to maintain a legal system in close harmony with EU law: for example by retaining in Scots law the Charter of Fundamental Rights of the European Union and by including in the bill a 'keeping pace' provision, empowering the Scottish Government to use secondary legislation to give effect to EU law after Brexit. What followed the bill's introduction was one of the most 'legalised' political episodes in the Parliament's history.

At the outset, the Presiding Officer (having received legal advice) stated his view that the bill was outside the legislative competence of the Parliament. His particular concern was the bill's provisions would empower the Scottish Parliament and Scottish Government to make changes to EU law – retained (devolved) EU law – after the UK's exit from the EU. He did not consider that the Parliament could take powers to take action at a future date – in this case to act contrary to EU law – where such action would be unlawful at the time the bill was introduced and/or passed.

The Lord Advocate – the Scottish Government's most senior law officer – responded by making a statement (acknowledged to be unprecedented) in Parliament explaining why in his view, and in the view of the Scottish Government, the bill was lawful. There followed detailed questions – from a range of MSPs beginning with Conservative MSP Adam Tompkins who holds the John Millar Chair of Public Law at the University of Glasgow – focused on the compatibility of the bill with the requirements of the Scotland Act. With respect to all those who asked questions one must assume that many MSPs had required detailed legal briefings to help them prepare for the debate.

Following the bill's passage at Stage 3 in March 2018, the UK Government took the rare step (a first for a Scottish bill) of asking the Supreme Court to rule on its lawfulness prior to royal assent. The effect of the request was to prevent the bill from becoming law pending the outcome of the case. In the meantime, the UK bill made progress at Westminster and just before it was finally passed it was amended so as to add itself to the list of Acts of the UK Parliament in Schedule 4 to the Scotland Act 1998 which may not be modified by the Scottish Parliament.

By the time the case was heard in July 2018, the UK Government's complaint was not only that the Scottish bill had been in some respects outside competence when it was passed but that by then it represented and attempt to modify the UK act and was unlawful for that reason. The judgment of the Supreme Court might be regarded as a 'score draw'. A number of challenges were dismissed, and others upheld space does not permit a full analysis here. However, the Supreme Court agreed that several provisions fell outside of legislative competence as a consequence of the supervening passage of the UK bill.

The Lord Advocate returned to the chamber to give a statement on the Supreme Court's ruling and took questions from MSPs: including again from Professor Tompkins and from Donald Cameron who made express mention of his membership of the Faculty of Advocates.

The ultimate impact of Brexit on devolution is yet to be fully understood. However, the changes that have been made to the Scotland Act 1998 by the European Union (Withdrawal) Act 2018 have the potential to create new legal challenges for the Scottish Parliament and for its members in understanding the scope of the Parliament's legislative competence. The following attempt to explain those in plain English no doubt highlights the problem.

As mentioned, the premise of the Scottish devolution scheme was that plenary legislative power is devolved subject only to specific limitations. Those limitations include the prohibition against laws that relate to reserved matters and the duty to comply with EU law. On the UK's departure from the EU it will no longer be necessary for the UK or indeed the Scottish Parliament to comply with EU law. An anticipated consequence was additional flexibility for the Scottish Parliament in devolved areas such as environmental, agricultural and public procurement law which are currently highly regulated by EU law.

The UK Government had and has concerns about the potential for the devolved administrations to opt for widely divergent regimes in some of these areas. As a result, the European Union (Withdrawal) Act 2018 empowers the UK Government, using secondary legislation, to prohibit the Scottish Parliament from changing 'retained EU law' (in essence the EU law that continues in force as a result of the 2018 act) in areas specified by the UK Government in regulations. If these powers are exercised, they will add a new dimension to the assessment of whether proposed legislation is within competence. Not only will it be necessary to understand whether the proposal relates to a matter that is devolved or reserved, it will also be necessary to analyse whether it modifies retained EU law – a concept which itself will be dynamic and is liable to change on an ongoing basis. Matters have the potential to become more complicated should the Scottish Parliament proceed to pass a new Continuity Bill.

What are the implications of this increasing complexity? I would be surprised if it leads to a significant increase in legal challenges to legislation by individuals or corporations. Such challenges are expensive and time consuming: challengers tend to have the benefit of legal aid or very substantial commercial resources. They are also, more often than not, unsuccessful. By contrast, and given the current political context, one might anticipate more frequent conflict in the courts between the UK Government and the devolved administrations in Scotland and elsewhere.

For those assisting our parliamentarians, there will be a need for them to provide increasingly detailed yet intelligible advice on questions of legislative competence. Such advice is already provided by the Office of the Solicitor to the Scottish Parliament (OSSP), with parliamentary legal advisers being involved in advising the Presiding Officer on legislative competence and in the passage of primary and secondary legislation. Their task – particularly where questions of competence become highly politicised within the Parliament itself – can only become more difficult.

For MSPs, the risk of getting it 'wrong' and facing challenge is a legal risk but one that faces the Parliament collectively. And, indeed, such challenges are defended not by the Parliament itself but by the Lord Advocate in the public interest as defender of the statute book. So far as political risk is concerned there is the potential for disaffection – on the part of MSPs and the public – if the work of the Parliament becomes increasingly dominated by debate about the extent of its legal powers rather than the exercise of those powers.

# CHAPTER 14

# The Scottish Economy:
# Fiscal Challenges and Opportunities

GRAEME ROY AND DAVID EISER

THE SCALE OF economic change in Scotland over the last 20 years has been striking. An initial period of strong growth gave way to the Great Recession, ushering in a period of weak growth in wages and living standards. Perhaps more striking than the scale of economic change has been the extent of the change in the Parliament's fiscal responsibilities. These changes, catalysed by the election of the first SNP government in 2007 and the 2014 independence referendum, have ushered in major new tax and welfare responsibilities for the Scottish Parliament. The devolved fiscal landscape is now far more complex than it was in 1999, with new institutions and the transfer of much greater risks.

The extent of policy change is arguably more mixed. In some areas, policy looks remarkably similar now as in 1999 (Council Tax and non-domestic rates for example). But elsewhere there have been major shifts in the distribution of spending, driven by a combination of demographics and the effects of fiscal austerity. What the next 20 years will hold is obviously uncertain. But with Brexit, and major structural shifts in our economy guaranteed, it is clearly going to be a period of further upheaval.

This chapter considers how the Scottish Parliament has responded to the economic and fiscal challenges over the first 20 years of devolution. It goes on to ask what the major economic and fiscal issues facing Scotland are likely to be over the next 20 years and assesses how well placed parliament might be to tackle them.

## Economic and Fiscal Policy Challenges of the Past 20 Years

The first eight years of the parliament, from 1999 to 2007, were characterised by a strongly performing economy (in Scotland and the UK) and a growing budget. Driven by a booming financial services industry, output per head in Scotland grew 20 per cent. Unemployment fell to just 4 per cent, with Scotland outperforming the UK on key employment measurements for the first time in decades. The resource block grant to finance day-to-day spending on public services increased by almost 50 per cent in real-terms (equivalent to around £9 billion).

After a rocky start, parliament began to play an effective role in scrutinising public policy but arguably had limited influence. Unsurprisingly, with Labour in power both at Holyrood and Westminster, public policy tended not to diverge markedly from the rest of the UK and where it did this tended to be because policy changes in England were not implemented in Scotland (eg tuition fees).

2007 marked the start of a turn towards a much weaker and less stable period for the economy and public finances. A year later, the global financial crisis had tipped Scotland into a sharp recession. In the end, the scale of the 2008-09 recession turned out to be smaller than perhaps many had feared. But the subsequent recovery has been unprecedently slow, with weak economic growth and limited pick up in living standards. Midway through 2018, output per head was only just over 2 per cent above its pre-crisis level. And whilst employment had risen to record levels, the combination of weak wage growth and cuts to in-work benefits means that for many households' real incomes are lower than they were back in 2008.

The programme of fiscal consolidation, commenced by the Labour Government, was strengthened by the Tory–Lib Dem coalition from 2010. Since then, the Scottish resource block grant has been cut by 7 per cent in real-terms. Of course, as well as marking a new economic era, 2007 marked political change, with the first SNP government. In response, the Unionist parties established the Calman Commission, which led to the partial devolution of Income Tax, and full devolution of landfill tax and stamp duty. By the time the commission's recommendations had become law in 2012, they had been overtaken by events.

The signing of the Edinburgh Agreement that same year fired the starting gun on a two-year debate on Scottish independence. The Parliament was inevitably pre-occupied with the referendum for much of the ensuing period. Whether it did a good job of informing the debate is open to question – although in many ways it was no different from general public life where the quality and tone of the economic and fiscal debate was poor. Where it has had greater success has been in scrutinising the transfer of fiscal powers and the establishment of new fiscal infrastructure. The Finance Committee played an important role for example in influencing the structure and independence of the Scottish Fiscal Commission.

The period since 2014 has again seen a shift in the key economic and fiscal challenges facing the Parliament. First, the Smith Commission recommendations, passed into legislation in 2016, have had far-reaching consequences both in terms of the Parliament's responsibilities and how policy is scrutinised. Second, the EU referendum in June 2016 has inevitably led to much debate around the authority of the Scottish Parliament, both in terms of the repatriation of economic powers from Brussels and the future role of Holyrood in UK-wide trade policy. Third, the sharp decline in the global oil price in late 2014 – from over $100 to just $30 a barrel in early 2016 – ushered in a period where Scottish economic performance has lagged behind the rest of the UK. Ironically this occurred just at a time when new tax powers were coming on stream that explicitly sought to better link Scottish economic performance with the Scottish budget.

The first of these themes, the transfer and operation of new fiscal powers, has been the key challenge for the parliament in the current session and will continue to dominate for the foreseeable future. As well as the new powers themselves, a new 'Fiscal Framework' was agreed by the Scottish and UK Governments. This sets out how devolved taxes and the block grant now interact to determine the Scottish budget. It also established new rules around borrowing and cash management to cope with the additional volatility and uncertainty arising from becoming more reliant on own-source tax revenues.

Ensuring a successful operational transfer of the powers, bringing transparency to the operation of the budget and scrutinising the Government's tax and spending policy, has created new challenges for the Parliament. It has responded by adopting a new budget process, with a year-round approach to scrutiny. This is justified partly by the complexity of the Fiscal Framework and the many moving parts that inform it (forecasts, tax outturn, reconciliations, and so on) and partly in an attempt to ensure that the Parliament can play more of a role in influencing policy. The revised process also includes scrutiny of the Government's medium-term budget planning, in an attempt to secure a renewed emphasis on strategic thinking about budget issues.

We remain in the early stages of the new framework and it remains unclear how effective the new processes will be. Air Passenger Duty has yet to be transferred, and VAT revenues are yet to be assigned. Most social security powers will be transferred in 2020–21 and 2021–22. Moreover, with a 15-month lag between the end of a financial year and outturn data we are yet to have been through a full budget cycle. Thus, the Scottish Government's new risk management tools have yet to be used in earnest.

In the main, the Parliament has had some limited success in bringing clarity to what is a much more complex set of budget arrangements, but there remains much work to be done to broaden public understanding. There must also be concern that budget debates are increasingly prone to become entrenched on the detail of relatively modest tax changes at the expense of debate on more fundamental and longer-term challenges and decisions. The Scottish budget faces major pressures going forward, and the Parliament has a critical role to play in articulating the challenges and opportunities that exist.

Beyond the big momentous events – referenda, recessions, new powers – how effective has the Parliament been in influencing and scrutinising economic and fiscal policy? A criticism sometimes levelled against Scottish economic and fiscal policy is that it has a tendency to be relatively timid. Whilst bold reforms are evident in other areas (for example the smoking ban and minimum unit pricing for alcohol), policy in the economic sphere has only tended to diverge materially from the UK when Scotland has opted for the *status quo* rather than responding to UK change – think the abolition of Regional Development Agencies or the introduction of undergraduate tuition fees in England. A possible exception to this was the 'Fresh Talent' programme introduced in 2005 that arose from parliamentary consensus of the need for a differentiated approach to addressing population in decline in Scotland.

Recently there has been a tendency to see some policy divergence in relation to tax policy. But economically and fiscally speaking, most of the changes have been marginal (although they are not necessarily framed that way in political and media discourse). And on big tax issues, the Parliament has shied away from bold reform. For example, despite an apparent parliamentary majority in favour of a new local tax to replace the Council Tax, the Parliament seems reluctant to get to grips with the reality of reform.

The Scottish Government's approach to economic policy strategy-building has also tended to remain somewhat timid. From an economics perspective, the latest iterations of the Scottish Government Economic Strategies (2007, 2011 and 2015) share much of substance with the preceding Framework for Economic Development (2004) and Smart, Successful Scotland (2001 and 2004). At the same time, the consensual approach to policy-making adopted has much to recommend it but has led to a plethora of sub-strategies, advisory groups and agencies. Whether this so-called 'cluttered landscape' helps the Parliament in its scrutiny role or makes it more difficult to progress against key challenges is a moot point.

One area where the Parliament has failed to hold government to account is in evaluating whether or not any of its strategies, advisory boards or initiatives have had the desired impact. Each Programme for Government, party conference or draft budget is typically accompanied by a 'new' initiative, backed up by investment and support from a collection of business organisations and/or government advisers. But the lack of subsequent evaluation and scrutiny of whether any of these initiatives have any real impact remains the weakest aspect of the economic policy landscape.

Where the Parliament has added value has been through a relentless demand for more and better data. There has been a substantial improvement in the level and availability of economic statistics, enabling a more nuanced understanding of Scottish economic trends than was possible in 1999. The outcome of the Economy, Jobs and Fair Work Committee's push to abolish Pre-Release Access privileges for Scottish ministers for Scottish economic and fiscal data will be a good test of the relative strength of parliament to force the Government to respond to the will of MSPS.

Budget scrutiny has been a mixed success. Parliament has brought transparency to some parts of the budget process, and driven improvements in the level of information provided. But in general, the parliament has had a limited role in influencing government spending plans, as had been envisaged when parliament was established. It has had some success in stimulating debate on the immediate effects of individual budgets, but a limited emphasis on highlighting the longer-term impacts and implications of successive budget decisions. Indeed, the Parliament has failed to force the Government to do any more than set out a one-year budget for the last five years or to take bolder reforms around the focus upon budgets driven by outcomes. The new budget process, and crucially the scrutiny of the Government's medium-term financial outlook, aims to tackle this.

## Future Economic and Fiscal Challenges

What is the next 20 years likely to hold, and how well placed is the parliament to tackle these issues? In the relatively short-term, there will be a number of important issues to resolve in relation to the Fiscal Framework. During the next two financial years we will see the first of the Income Tax 'reconciliations' (the reckoning between the tax forecasts that were made when budgets were set with the reality of the outturn data). These will expose the extent to which the existing borrowing and cash management tools are adequate or require reform. An important decision will also be required on the question of whether the proposal to assign VAT revenues to the Scottish budget should go ahead in 2020–21 given the emergence of significant uncertainties in the estimation of these revenues and the consequent budgetary risks.

The Parliament's role in this respect should be to bring transparency and clarity to what are often complex issues around statistical uncertainty and what this implies for budgetary risks and the funding of public services. These issues will lie at the heart of the renegotiation of the Fiscal Framework which is scheduled to take place towards the end of 2021. Whilst ostensibly a matter for inter-governmental negotiation, it will be essential that the Parliament has oversight of and can influence these negotiations, drawing on its experiences of scrutinising and communicating the impacts of the Fiscal Framework during this parliamentary session. If the inter-governmental negotiations around the existing Fiscal Framework are anything to go by, then it seems quite likely that negotiations will undoubtedly hit various impasses along the way. The Parliament should be able to play a role in informing and unlocking these blockages, although its ability to do so will depend on the openness of the Governments as to the status of negotiations. The Parliament should also seek to ensure that it inputs to, and is informed by, the independent review of the Fiscal Framework that the Governments have committed to in advance of renegotiation.

Thinking beyond the Fiscal Framework in a narrow sense, there is some justifiable concern that the focus of the Finance Committee in scrutinising tax forecasts and tax policy leaves a gap in relation to spending choices and trends. Whilst subject committees scrutinise the implications of spending decisions for their respective portfolios, it is not clear where the scrutiny of broader spending choices takes place; nor who will now drive the strategic context to budget scrutiny, such as the focus on a preventative approach or whether the budget stacks up against the wider outcomes agenda as set out in the National Performance Framework.

At some point too, politicians will need to confront the apparent inertia around reform of local taxation, and what can be done to unlock this blockage. 13 years after the Burt Review and four years after the Commission on Local Tax Reform, there appears to remain a consensus that the current system is not fit for purpose, although parliament's willingness to instigate and drive change remains muted.

Beyond these relatively concrete fiscal issues that we can be relatively certain about, the Parliament is likely to face a range of other economic and fiscal challenges, some of which we can be relatively certain about and others over which there is more uncertainty.

On one level, those that thought that devolution would lead to a transformation of Scotland's long-term economic fortunes will be disappointed. Scotland continues to remain the wealthiest part of the UK outside of London and has had notable successes in areas such as renewable energy and attracting international investment.

But in many other areas, the economic challenges that Scotland faced 20 years ago remain today. Our productivity remains some 20 per cent below the best performing OECD countries, despite a target to match them by 2017. Our export base is much smaller than that of our competitors, with a target to boost our international exports by 50 per cent between 2010 and 2017 missed by nearly 15 percentage points. On R&D, almost 40 per cent of such expenditure is attributable to just five companies with Scotland ranking 8th out of the 12 devolved nations and English regions of the UK. On new business start-ups, Scotland ranks 10th, and also lags behind the UK average in terms of levels of entrepreneurship and innovation.

Our economy remains heavily unbalanced geographically. Average income in North Ayrshire is a fraction of that in Edinburgh. The 16–64 employment rate is as high as 80 per cent in Aberdeenshire, but as low as

66 per cent in Dundee and Glasgow. And for all the talk about 'inclusive growth', nearly one million people – including nearly one in four children – live in poverty.

The fallout from the Great Recession and fiscal austerity has arguably limited parliament's ability to effectively debate and offer new ideas on how to address these challenges. Indeed, recent events have only illustrated that – in many key areas – the major macroeconomic and fiscal policy levers remain at Westminster. But many of Scotland's long-term challenges lie within devolved powers. If Scotland is to turn around many of these indicators it is likely to require a boldness in policy that we have yet to see in the last 20 years.

Of course, all of this will be overshadowed – at least in the short-term – by the fallout from Brexit. Parliament has shown itself largely powerless to alter the course of UK policy, even after the refusal to give consent for Westminster's Withdrawal Bill. To be fair, much of this stems from a lack of any coherent plan for Brexit at the UK level and increased levels of mistrust between the Scottish and UK Governments. Whatever the final outcome, it is clear that Holyrood's economic and fiscal responsibilities will change after Brexit.

The question of how funding for aspects of agri-environment policy might be allocated has been touched on by various parliamentary committees but will at some point demand significant scrutiny. Hopes for differentiated policy in areas such as migration and international trade are likely to be blocked but deserve to be considered. And the replacement of EU Structural Funds, which have boosted spending on infrastructure and social programmes across Scotland, will also need to be reviewed, implemented and assessed. The risks to Holyrood's budget are high.

The major 'known' long-term economic shift over the next 20 years which will have a profound effect both on the Scottish economy and public finances is demographic change, colloquially referred to as 'population ageing'. The number of people aged over 75 is expected to increase by 79 per cent over the next 25 years. This process of population ageing will continue to have profound implications for the distribution of public spending. Scottish Government spending on health has risen from 37 per cent of day-to-day devolved spending in 1999–2000 to 48 per cent in 2019–20 and is set to continue on this trajectory into the medium-term. Local government spending on social care for older aged adults is similarly absorbing a larger and larger share of local government spending.

These trends have profound implications for the quality and extent of public service delivery in a raft of other areas.

It is essential that we have a more open and transparent debate about these trends and their implications. Is civic society content for recent changes in spending distribution to continue? Can we make more transparent, strategic and consensual decisions about which areas of public service delivery the public sector steps back from? At what point do we need to become realistic about the scope of additional public revenue raising required to meet ambitions for public service delivery?

Whilst we can be certain about the nature and likely magnitude of demographic change over the medium-term, other economic trends are associated with more uncertainty. Will Scotland be more or less impacted by Brexit than the rest of the UK? How will Scotland's economy cope with the long-term decline in the North Sea? And what are the risks and opportunities for Scotland's economy from the Fourth Industrial Revolution and the rise of the digital economy?

The next 20 years will undoubtedly see major changes to the Scottish economy. Some of these will announce themselves as major one-off events (often crises), whilst others will occur more gradually, perhaps almost imperceptibly. The former can include the effects of macroeconomic shocks which hit one or more industries, whilst the latter can include the effects of gradual labour market change arising as a result of changes in skills demand. The Parliament needs to be alert to both types of change and their implications – and where possible to be on the front-foot, enhancing economic resilience by preparing the economy for change before it has happened.

## Conclusions

A substantial change in the Scottish Parliament's fiscal responsibilities and financial accountability is underway, resulting in major evolution of budget process and the institutional landscape. This, together with the ongoing uncertainty around Brexit and possible further fiscal change as a result, will continue to be a major preoccupation of the parliament in the near future.

On a more permanent level, parliament will need to be in a position to articulate the big long-term economic and fiscal challenges and changes that are underway or likely. This includes both those challenges that we know relatively more about (demographic change) and those that we have less certainty about (how economic structural changes might affect skills demands and infrastructure needs). It needs to make its voice heard about the implications of these issues and the appropriate responses.

Making this happen in practice is, of course, more easily said than done. It requires, partly, a renewed emphasis on thinking about medium-term challenges, as much as on annual budget changes. This is something the new budget process seeks to catalyse through the introduction of annual scrutiny of the Government's five-year financial strategy. It remains too early to say how effective this new process will be, but it seems likely that there will be a need for strategic thinking about likely fiscal challenges in the future, as opposed to taking the Government's existing spending commitments and extrapolating those forward – useful as that is.

But long-term challenges and trends are likely to also require, more ambitiously, a more collegiate and cross-party approach, one that seeks consensus on the big issues, big questions and what should be done to understand their broad implications (although not necessarily the specific policy response).

It is impossible to say at this stage whether or not there will be another referendum on Scottish independence during the next 20 years. If and when it does happen, it would be unrealistic to expect parliamentarians to do anything other than to divide into two opposing camps. But we should hope that, learning from the divisive experiences of the 2014 independence referendum and 2016 EU referendum, a future debate will be underpinned by a greater willingness to accept the scale of uncertainties and complexities that underlie any assessment of the likely outcomes of different constitutional configurations. An independence debate would engage all civic society, and parliament has a critical role in setting the tone of any debate and the way it is conducted.

The next 20 years are likely to see economic change at least as significant as the past 20 years, as well as further significant change to the constitutional settlement. Policy-making and debate will increasingly need to focus on the medium- and longer-term outcomes of policy, and the inevitability of uncertainty and risk. We hope the Parliament will be able to rise to the challenge.

*Dear Scottish Parliament...*

As a young person living in Scotland, here are some improvements I would like to see the Scottish Parliament make: working together, not against each other, to better the lives of Scottish people and those living in Scotland.

Working to tackle and eradicate major problems such as homelessness and substance abuse and dependency. A way to tackle the major issue that is substance abuse would be to introduce an informative or educational programme that is delivered to children from an early age, so they understand the effects and know how to seek help.

Ensuring every child in Scotland has a loving and supportive environment for them to grow up in and if a child doesn't have a loving family ensuring there are alternative care options where they will feel safe and wanted.

Another example would be, introducing a fair and just benefits system that would lift families out of poverty and provide them with necessities they need. Rather than reacting to problems, intervene earlier.

Let the voices of *all* the young people in Scotland be heard to give them the future *they* desire instead of the future picked out for them by previous generations.

Provide rehabilitation centres for not only substance abuse but also for things such as eating disorders and mental health issues. Provide accessible help for people, especially young people, suffering from mental health disorders.

Imagine a Scotland where everyone is accepted, a Scotland where everyone has a home and a family to support them. Imagine a Scotland where everyone has a smile on their face and feels safe. Imagine a Scotland where young people are happy with the world handed down before them. Imagine a Scotland where no one has to sleep on the streets. Imagine this Scotland. This is the Scotland that I want. This is the Scotland that we want. This is the Scotland you need to deliver.

*Quinn Muirhead, 14, West Lothian*

CHAPTER 15

# Principles and Practices of the Good Parliament

## Babyleave, Institutional Resistance and Change

SARAH CHILDS

I'M SITTING ACROSS from a senior male Labour MP in his office in Portcullis House. I can't take in quickly enough or effectively respond to what he has just said. I am momentarily floored. This was an MP who I assumed would be sympathetic – I'd taken soundings; it was why I was meeting him. His words were cutting: *I* would be creating a scandal; *I* would be making things worse for women MPs; there was *no* problem. We were discussing what would become Recommendation 12 of 'The Good Parliament Report'. It made the Commons Reference Group on Representation and Inclusion – a new group of MPs established in the wake of the report's publication – responsible for producing a 'House Statement' on maternity and paternity leave. The Labour male MP's unexpected, accusatory outburst made me temporarily question my reading of the institution.

The pregnant MP makes individual and informal arrangements for any leave. And whilst I was fully prepared to concede that this was mostly a workable arrangement – women MPs are given time off using the long-standing system of 'pairing' – it was not good enough. Symbolically it was failing to be inclusive of a large proportion of the population; substantively the House was failing to accommodate its own members. At the individual level it moreover infantilised the woman MP who had to ask for her 'maternity leave'; leave that was dependent upon the predilection of the Whips. History tells us that when the parliamentary numbers require it MPs are required to return to the House to vote, as the award-winning play *This House* so effectively dramatized. More than this, an informal and opaque arrangement leaves MPs vulnerable to misrepresentation. The mother MP ends up at the bottom of voting league tables; the media raise questions about her quality and effectiveness.

My Labour male MP's concern was not mainly for the mother MP, however. His hostility was based more on the claim that by introducing a formal system of maternity leave I would put at risk the privacy of the 'ill MP' who might not wish to disclose the reasons why they were, on a particular occasion or over a period of time, 'paired'. If I had been (embarrassingly) unable to immediately refute his elision between pregnancy and illness, I was at least much more conscious of parliamentary resistance, even amongst those MPs who I had thought of as broadly sympathetic.

As I would subsequently come to recognise, arguments about the effectiveness of existing practices frequently camouflage what are MPs' preferences. That said, I was sure as I drafted my report that redressing the institutional failure to provide for the mother MP could not be side-stepped. Babyleave was to be one of 43 recommendations in 'The Good Parliament'. I had not been persuaded by a senior official's suggestion that I limit its remit to identifying the 'top' three or four issues, as if resolving these would be sufficient to make the institution 'better'.

## Diversity Sensitive Parliaments

'The Good Parliament Report' resulted from a full-time secondment to the House of Commons, dating from late summer 2015 until late spring 2016. The first task was to document the House's gender insensitivities. As one of my external advisors who had previously worked in the Commons made clear, I must convince MPs of this. I should do so as parsimoniously as possible, and not in an academic way. Table 1, a 'Red, Amber, Green' account of how well or badly the House was doing was informed by the Inter-Parliamentary Union's (IPU's) Gender Sensitive Parliaments framework and (quietly) drew upon more than a decade of feminist scholarship on gender and UK politics, parties and parliament. If the table itself was rarely contested, my focus on gender soon was. An initial outline of my project to the House of Commons Commission, gave rise to concerns from some male MPs. A gender focus was negatively perceived as privileging women: 'did I not know that men had families too?', one MP asked. I adopted an explicitly 'diversity sensitive' framework in part to pre-empt further such criticism.

TABLE I

'RAG' Analysis of the UK House of Commons:
Representation and Inclusions

| DIMENSION | MEASURE | RED | AMBER | GREEN |
|---|---|---|---|---|
| EQUALITY OF PARTICIPATION | Diversity of MPs | X | | |
| | Women's House leadership positions | X | | |
| | Women's participation (internal structures; committees) | | X | |
| INFRASTRUCTURE | Standing Orders | | X | |
| | Calendar & sitting hours | X | | |
| | Equalities & diversity body (policy) | | | X |
| | Equalities & diversity body (institutional) | X | | |
| | Parliamentary buildings & spaces | | X | |
| | Childcare & child-friendly provisions | | X | |
| | Maternity & parental leave | X | | |
| CULTURE | House commitment & action plan | X | | |
| | Chamber culture (PMQs & 'set-pieces') | X | | |

Once the report was handed over, the House of Commons could no longer claim that it was not aware of what needed to be done, nor claim ignorance of possible solutions. Each recommendation was technically accurate, in large part due to my advisory group of House officials. Political feasibility was informed by an MPs' panel. Each recommendation was also explicitly linked to particular individuals and groups within the Commons, in an attempt to assign responsibility and increase the chances of implementation. Overarching institutional leadership would be provided by the new Commons Reference Group. It first met in autumn 2016 with cross-party membership and comprising women and men MPs to reflect the commitment to 'diversity sensitivity'. At an early meeting the group requested a short description of 'The Good House of Commons'. I described such an institution in the following fashion:

For members, the public visitor, for those coming on Parliamentary business, and for staff, is one that is *truly representative*. Members, staff and visitors would reflect the major social characteristics of those the House represents. The ambition to participate in, and the resources needed for, politics are evenly distributed throughout society; barriers to participation have been removed. Political parties have put in place supply and demand side mechanisms to ensure that MPs are diverse. The House's activities and its structures – committee members and chairs, expert witnesses, clerks and House staff – are representative too. Interactions between MPs and staff are of the highest standards of professionalism.

*Transparent*. Whether member, staff or visitor, all are confident in their knowledge of the work of MPs and of the institution as whole, recognise the enabling work of staff, and the democratic role the public play in parliament. House procedures, practices and norms are straightforward; traditions that mystify have been removed. The people who populate the House look in their dress and in the manner of their interactions like those outside.

*Accessible*. This is both physical and psychological: there is a strong sense of belonging and efficacy amongst all who work in or who attend the House. There is no longer a single image of who the MP, the senior Clerk, or the 'important' parliamentary visitor is. Technology enables greater engagement. Children are welcome. The physical needs of all who work in or come into the House are met. MPs are entitled to parental and caring leave; the business costs and expenses scheme supports members' in both of their places of work, the constituency and Westminster.

*Accountable and effective*. Greater certainty over the scheduling of parliamentary business, and with 'core business hours', means that MPs have more control over, and flexibility in, how they do their job.

MPS and staffs' work-life balance are improved. The House's performance is maximised, free from sexism and sexual harassment, racism, disabilism, homophobia and classism. In interactions between MPs, officials and the public substantive gains will come from hearing the widest possible set of views. Notably, committee witnesses would be diverse, ensuring that in holding government to account, MPs are receiving a full range of perspectives. Institutional attention to diversity and equality is guaranteed by the now permanent Women and Equalities Committee, and the Commons Reference Group on Representation and Inclusion, ensuring that all interests are addressed.

In sum 'The Good House of Commons' is one that is a globally acknowledged, best practice 'diversity sensitive' House.

In the nearly three years since publication, 11 recommendations have been implemented in part or in full: (1) children are now permitted in the division lobbies; (2) there has been provision of additional childcare; (3) the dress code has been revised (4) the Commission accepted its collective responsibility for representation and inclusion; (5) Select Committee witness diversity data is now monitored; (6) the parliamentary pass has been redesigned to make it double-sided; (7) the IPU undertook a gender audit of both Houses of Parliament; (8) the 'ten-year dead rule' for artwork (the artist must be dead for ten years before their art work can be used) in the Palace has been abolished; (9) a gender balance quota for a new select committee was passed; (10) the Women and Equalities Committee was made permanent; and (11) proxy voting for babyleave was introduced. Other recommendations are ongoing: monitoring MPs' participation in speeches; provisions for greater Lobby journalist diversity; norms of parliamentary behaviour have become part of wider discussions about bullying and harassment; and House statements promoting the role and work of MPs are in development.

## Proxy Voting for Babyleave

Despite a principled rejection of ranking recommendations in the report itself, the Reference Group considered Recommendation 12 a priority, and a likely 'quick win'. A survey of a select sample of comparable parliaments showed that *six* had formal babyleave arrangements (Australia;

Denmark; Finland; Germany; New Zealand; and Spain), *four* relied on informal party arrangements (Canada, Scotland, Wales, Westminster) and *one* – Sweden – matched their country-level provision. The UK Parliament was behind not only Scandinavia as might be expected, but also Australia and New Zealand, Commonwealth comparators that I was advised UK MPs took seriously. The Reference Group worked closely with the newly entitled Mother of the House, the Rt Hon Harriet Harman MP, who had made babyleave her first priority. Together, a motion was put before the House and agreed in February 2018. The Procedure Committee was tasked to report how proxy voting could be made to work in practice, which it swiftly did. A second debate was held in September 2018, albeit one that had no voteable motion. I suspect that some male MPs had not realised that the House had voted in principle for proxy voting earlier in the year; there was now concern that the second debate would mobilise the antis. The Leader of the House Andrea Leadsom was adamant she was committed to introducing a voteable motion in the autumn of 2018; it failed to materialise. Some of this had to do with the time spent on debating Brexit, but there were also suspicions that the delay was linked to the antipathy of Whips. With very tight votes looming, pregnant MPs and their supporters were clear that there could be no more delay.

Two or perhaps three incidents seemed to prompt the January 2019 vote. First, the system of pairing was increasingly perceived as unreliable. In July 2018, the Conservative MP Brandon Lewis voted when he was paired with the Liberal Democrat Jo Swinson, whose baby was then just a few weeks old. Second, the Labour MP Tulip Siddiq delayed her caesarean so that she could vote in one of the Brexit votes. Images of the heavily pregnant MP in a wheelchair in the Chamber were telling of an institution antithetical to the mother (-to-be) MP, to say the least. Third, and this is disputed, the media reported that a key obstacle was the Conservative Chief Whip. Urgent questions were allowed by Mr Speaker. Babyleave was making the news and the symbols were all wrong. Late at night, a one-year pilot proxy voting scheme for babyleave was finally approved by the House without a division. MPs – male and female – have since used proxies during subsequent Brexit votes, leading to suggestions that the 'Cooper Bill' would have been lost without this change to the House's rules.

## Institutional Change

Whilst parliaments are not unchanging institutions, they are rarely easy to change. Historically designed for, and by men, many parliaments have simply never properly considered the needs of the women MP. The parent MP – mother and father – has been considered even less, despite fathers having always been present. Mainstream political science accounts mostly fail to consider questions of gender and diversity when considering institutional change; it has been left to feminist political science and international organisations (and their gender activists therein), namely the IPU, the UN, and the European Institute for Gender Equality to identify the ways in which gender saturates our political institutions and to expand definitions of parliamentary effectiveness in terms of representation and inclusion.

Key to feminist accounts of institutional re-gendering are a parliament's gender-conscious actors – usually assumed to be elected women members. Women MPs were indeed critical to the development of 'The Good Parliament Report' and were often both its and my champion within the House then, and since its critical actors. But the Report also benefitted from others on both the political and official side. The latter are rarely acknowledged in extant theories of institutional change. Critical male allies on the political side notably included Mr Speaker, the Rt Hon John Bercow, and members of my MPs advisory board. On the official side, a number of senior male clerks provided the technical insights that I needed to draft the recommendations. One provided sustained in-depth guidance and offered critical, albeit encouraging, comment. Another fundamental relationship was with a mid-ranking female official – 'my feminist in residence' – whose own feminist commitment helped me better read the gender politics of the institution.

In reviewing the successful recommendations from 'The Good Parliament', critics might query the significance of changing the rules about what MPs can wear or whether it matters that the misogynistic 'ten-year dead' artwork rule has been abolished. The choices that have been made regarding which to prioritise reflect both the priorities of the Reference Group's membership and theirs and Mr Speaker's capacity to lead on particular reforms. It was *his* decision *vis à vis* parliamentary attire, and also his permission that allows children into the division lobbies and babies in the Chamber. Recommendations where the House (ie members) need to agree via a vote or a resolution of the House, and, or where the Government needed to act, have admittedly proven harder to achieve. To be clear, there has also been failure. The most notable of which – not least because 2018 was the centenary year of the first women gaining the right to vote and sit in the House – was Recommendation 22, which provided for the enactment of Section 106 of the Equality Act 2010. This requires political parties to publish parliamentary candidate diversity data. There is no reason not to enact Section 106 other than the Government wishes to resist it. Stronger recommendations relating to parliamentary sex quotas (Sections 8 and 9) were tellingly not even a serious target for most campaigners, such is their rejection by most Conservatives.

'The Good Parliament Report' offered the UK House of Commons a 'shopping bag' of reforms. As written elsewhere, I never expected the Commons Reference Group to have achieved what it has in its short life. An institutionalisation of its agenda across the Commons' political and official sides, and indeed to the Lords is observable. The 2018 IPU Gender Sensitive Audit of both Houses was a conscious attempt to ensure that parliament undertook a formal review of its progress two years after the Report's publication. Another two years or so and it will be timely to undertake a second audit, hopefully adopting a diversity sensitive framework. Some reforms look secure. There is much confidence that babyleave will become a permanent feature at the end of its pilot year, for example. Others less so. There is plenty of concern at Westminster that old habits are returning.

The parliamentary politics of Brexit undoubtedly displaced and disrupted 'normal' parliamentary business and made for new political fault-lines, over and above general institutional tendencies to preserve themselves. The last two years have also been a time where questions of the House's culture, organisation and leadership has been much criticised, and which mediated and, at times limited, the actions of the Reference Group. Restoration and Renewal of the Palace could be a moment of opportunity if it were to be grasped, but conservatism again appears to be the main tendency. There is also the question of Bercow's successor: if the Speaker election becomes framed in terms of modernisation versus tradition, as well it might, then some recent gains may very well come under threat. I suspect that those gender-conscious actors identified as key to institutional re-gendering by academic researchers – women MPs, women officials, extra-parliamentary actors in the media, academia and think tanks as well as their male allies

– would become vocal opponents of any parliamentary dinosaurs that seek to turn the clock metaphorically, and perhaps literally, back.

If 'The Good Parliament' recommendations are specific to the UK House of Commons, its framework and approach can travel. A companion survey of parliaments, including Holyrood and the National Assembly for Wales, brought together new data on select areas of parliamentary best and poor practice. But there is much comparative analysis to be undertaken. There can and should be inter-institutional lesson-learning: parliaments are linked at the political and official level – with Speakers, Clerks and officials, and groups of MPs engaged in a number of international and national groupings and organisations. In late summer 2018, parliamentary delegations from Westminster and Holyrood – members and officials – joined academics from England, Scotland, Sweden, and Catalonia at the Parliament de Catalunya to examine their 'gender equality plan' strategy. As the IPU maintains, political institutions should be truly representative, transparent, accessible, accountable and effective in all their functions. Globally, gender equality and diversity activists in parliaments, academia and civil society are rightly working together to ensure that our individual parliaments, and parliaments collectively, meet this international standard.

*Dear Scottish Parliament...*

I hope that in the next 20 years there will be more girls in the engineering world as this is what I would like to do when I'm older so it would be great if there would be more girls taking the lead in engineering. I would also like to see more girls in computing jobs as there are not many girls doing engineering and science.

What I would also like to see in the next 20 years is an overhaul of the way Parliament/Government is run due to the digital age that we now live in. Millions could be saved every year on expenses that could be replaced with Skype or FaceTime and MSP second homes abolished.

In the next 20 years I would like to see sports opportunities available to every child in Scotland and not just the children whose parents can afford it as my own personal experiences are to be a champion in any sport and make it to the top. If you don't have the financial backing of your parents, then regardless of talent the child will never make it to the top. I would like to see more kids from a disadvantaged background with talent become successful champions.

I would also like to see Scotland lead the way in innovation, ideas and inventions. Scotland has so much to offer, we should do more in renewable energies and become a world leader.

I would like to see Scotland's tourism increase and our vast beautiful landscape become world knowledge which in turn will increase revenue and income to Scotland which would be good for our economy and Scotland becomes recognised worldwide for our picture-perfect scenery.

*Robyn Gibson, 14, West Lothian*

# CHAPTER 16

# Look, Listen

## This is Who We Are

### JAMES ROBERTSON

IN *MAID IN WAITING*, a late novel by that always astute chronicler of the English upper middle-class John Galsworthy, the following exchange occurs:

> 'Parliament now is just a taxing machine.'
> 'Surely it still makes laws?'
> 'Yes, my dear; but always after the event; it consolidates what has become public practice, or at least public feeling. It never initiates. How can it? That's not a democratic function.'

The year is 1928 and the speakers are two women in their 20s (so, enfranchised by the Representation of the People Act of that year). The first speaker, Fleur – daughter of Soames Forsyte – suggests, not necessarily approvingly, that with the arrival of 'one person, one vote' the relationship between Westminster and the public has changed for ever. Parliament now has to reflect and respond to what the people want of it rather than impose its legislative will on them.

Seven decades later, in the non-fictional political world, the bill that would create a modern Scottish Parliament was introduced at Westminster. In December 1997 Donald Dewar, Secretary of State for Scotland in the new Labour Government, read out the opening sentence of the Scotland Bill: 'There shall be a Scottish Parliament'. 'I like that,' he added, and it was clear from the understated way he said it how much he meant it. He continued:

> In well under three hundred days we have set in train the biggest change in three hundred years of Scottish history... Everything that is not reserved comes to Edinburgh. The people asked us to deliver a Scottish Parliament – that is exactly what we will do. And that's a promise.

As we know, the promise was kept. As we also know, a parliament –
Fleur Forsyte's opinion notwithstanding – *is* more than just a taxing
machine. In a representative democracy, arguably, a parliament has three
principal roles: to make laws; to represent the people who elect its members; and to monitor the actions of the Executive and hold it to account
through oversight, inquiry and debate. It is remarkable how used we
already are to the way the Scottish Parliament does these things, how familiar we have become with its elections (five of them to date), and how
smoothly, on the whole, its procedures work. The 'new' political landscape looks remarkably mature after only 20 years. Apart from those few
who remain viscerally and resolutely opposed to devolution, would any
politician now seriously propose flattening that landscape and returning
it to how it was before? Would any party openly campaign in a Scottish election to reduce the powers that have passed from Westminster to
Holyrood? Would any incoming Scottish Government, of whatever hue,
opt to change its title back to 'Scottish Executive'? Only, perhaps, if it
also intended to reinstate tolls on the country's road bridges, cancel the
smoking in public spaces ban and legalise bear-baiting. If devolution is,
in Enoch Powell's phrase, power retained, it is also power acquired. Or
again, as Ron Davies, Secretary of State for Wales, memorably put it in
1997, 'devolution is a process, not an event'.

Why do we have a Parliament in Edinburgh? Because in the 1980s
and 1990s a majority of the Scottish electorate came to believe that it
was both desirable and necessary. They reached this conclusion, and voted for it, because they felt that the existing UK model of representative
democracy was not working properly; that the Westminster Parliament
did not fairly or accurately represent the Scottish people's will; that it did
not always make laws that were in Scotland's best interests and often
enacted government policies that were inimical to the expressed will of
most Scots. There was also a sense that Westminster was not equipped to
hold the Scottish Office, a department of the UK Government, to account;
that in the late 20th century neither the mechanisms nor the motivation
to do this properly existed, if they ever had. It was widely felt, in other
words – especially after 18 years of rule by Conservative Governments
which had been repeatedly rejected by the Scottish electorate – that a
serious democratic deficit existed in the way Scotland was governed and
treated and that the establishment of a devolved legislature in Edinburgh
would go some way to reducing that deficit. This feeling went far beyond

individual politicians or political parties: the campaign for a Parliament (which began in the wake of the 1979 referendum with the formation of the Campaign for a Scottish Assembly) was an alliance of various parties, civic groups, churches, trade unions and local government representatives as well as individuals with a wide range of cultural, commercial, academic and practical interests and experience.

Some, of course, voted for devolution in September 1997 hoping it would be a stepping-stone to independence; others voted for it believing it was a positive development in itself but that it would, additionally, make the case for independence redundant. There was a gut feeling underlying the vote, however, which I think was shared by both these groups: if a time came again, as it surely would, when Scotland's politics did not align with the politics of a UK Government, then a Scottish Parliament would be a legitimate locus where that difference could be asserted. It would be a line of political defence that had been sorely missed in the 1980s and 1990s and before. The Parliament, that is, would give Scotland a political voice that had been absent not just in those decades, but for nearly three centuries.

The period following the Brexit referendum of June 2016 has proved to be the most obvious context for measuring how loud that voice might be. When, for example, on 5 December 2018, all the parties at Holyrood, other than the Scottish Conservatives, backed a motion rejecting both Prime Minister Theresa May's withdrawal plan and the prospect of leaving the European Union without a deal, they were effectively asserting the Parliament's right not only to dissent from, but also to challenge, the UK Government's policy. A week later, the Supreme Court ruled on the legitimacy of the Scottish Parliament's UK Withdrawal from the European Union (Legal Continuity) (Scotland) Bill, which it had approved in April 2018 despite a warning from the Presiding Officer Ken Macintosh that it might be acting *ultra vires*. This ruling followed a lengthy court battle between the senior law officers of the Scottish and UK Governments. Although the Supreme Court did indeed rule that some provisions of the bill were out with the legal competence of the Scottish Parliament – principally because it would modify the European Union (Withdrawal) Act at Westminster, which had become law by the time the case was heard – the interpretation of this judgment by the two sides differed widely. Before devolution, this kind of legal and constitutional wrangling simply would not have been played out in public, if at all, and had such arguments been aired at Westminster any united front of Scottish opposition parties would have been outvoted by the governing party there.

It should not be forgotten, in all this, that the creation of the Scottish Parliament, and in particular its voting system, rescued the Scottish Conservative Party from near-oblivion after the elimination of all its Scottish MPs at Westminster in the 1997 general election. It is currently the largest opposition party at Holyrood. The pre-devolution democratic deficit applied as much to the Scottish Tories, in this respect, as it did to Scotland as a whole. Neither should it be forgotten that the Scottish National Party, which has benefited most from the Parliament's establishment, did not participate in the Constitutional Convention which drew up and in 1995 published 'Scotland's Parliament, Scotland's Right', the blueprint for devolution.

On the Canongate wall of the Parliament, alongside many other literary quotations, is inscribed part of a sentence from Walter Scott's great novel of 1818, *The Heart of Midlothian*. In this story, set in 1736 nearly 30 years after the old Scottish Parliament voted itself out of existence, Scott depicted widespread dissatisfaction among Edinburgh's citizens at what had been lost. The full sentence, delivered by the character Mrs Howden, is as follows:

> I dinna ken muckle about the law... but I ken, when we had a king, and a chancellor, and parliament-men o' our ain, we could aye peeble them wi' stanes when they werena gude bairns – But naebody's nails can reach the length o' Lunnon.

In these few, fictional words Scott captured something essentially true about how most people relate to the mechanisms through which they are governed. They care little about how the system works, but they do care if it doesn't work, or is so remote as to seem ignorant or dismissive of their lives. No doubt some would say that Holyrood is no more concerned about them than Westminster, and no doubt in some places Edinburgh feels almost as remote as London. But there has been a shift in public consciousness since 1999, a recognition that politics has been brought home and that as a result there is greater accessibility to our representatives and to the workings of government. We do have better contact with our MSPs, and we can, at least metaphorically, peeble them wi stanes. The option of using real stanes is, of course, always there, as it was in 1736.

It is often said that the debate over independence in 2014 provoked greater levels of public engagement with politics than anybody, anywhere in the UK, could recall. The turnout at the referendum of that year was an astonishing 85 per cent of registered voters. That referendum came about, however, only because the political landscape had been changed so significantly by the creation, or re-creation, of a parliament in Edinburgh. That brought existential questions about what Scotland was – a partner in union, a stateless nation, a nation-state in waiting? – to the fore and into focus. The overall majority achieved by the SNP in 2011 – something which the additional member electoral system was supposed to make almost impossible – made the referendum inevitable, but the groundwork for it had been laid when Donald Dewar said, 'There shall be a Scottish Parliament'. Devolution did not 'kill nationalism stone dead' as George Robertson predicted in 1995. Whether, as the late Tam Dalyell believed, it is a motorway to independence with no exits remains to be seen – and depends at least as much on events elsewhere as it does on Scotland's domestic politics.

A cautionary note here: turnout at Scottish parliamentary elections has never been higher than 59 per cent, and at three of them it has hovered around the 50 per cent mark. These turnout figures are approximately 10 per cent lower than for UK general elections, a difference open to various explanations but which certainly doesn't suggest greater enthusiasm for engagement with Scottish than with UK politics. On the other hand, there is no strong evidence that Scottish voters are more apathetic or less interested than their Welsh or English counterparts, or indeed than voters in other countries.

The first Scottish Parliament since 1707 met on 12 May 1999. If one accepts the dubious notion – powerfully articulated by Winnie Ewing MSP on that day – that this was the old Scottish Parliament woken from centuries of slumber, it was 'reconvened'. It was not, of course: the new Parliament looked and behaved nothing like the old one, even in the years before it settled in its new custom-built home at the foot of the Royal Mile. In many respects, it was also unlike the Parliament at Westminster which had brought it into existence – notably in the way its members were elected. Over the next two decades those differences became more marked, as the political priorities and choices of the constituent parts of the United Kingdom also diverged. Watching or listening to the UK 'national' news today, I am often struck by the feeling that I am receiving reports from a foreign country. This is not a delusion: increasingly, they do things differently there.

The preparation done by the Constitutional Convention, the pre-existence of a separate and functioning Scottish legal system, and the emphatic endorsement of the people in the two-question referendum of 1997, made the process of establishing the Parliament quicker and easier than it might otherwise have been. The Scottish Parliamentary Service, led during these 20 years by its Chief Executive Sir Paul Grice, must also take much of the credit for maintaining the smoothness of the procedural road surface during challenging political times. As Sir Paul wrote in an article (15 July 2016) in the magazine *Holyrood*, 'Our aim was straightforward; to be a credible operation from day one'. In this, despite severe stresses such as the cost and time overruns in constructing the new building or the setting-up of a regulatory system for MSPs' expenses, he and his team succeeded. The Scots are neither uniquely incapable nor uniquely gifted in getting political and administrative change right, and it is only with the passage of time that what seemed near-disasters can be seen in proper perspective. In that same article, Sir Paul made some further points:

The Scottish Parliament began to build a reputation for innovation: one of the first in the world to have a dedicated public petitions committee; a strong focus on novel and imaginative public engagement; and extensive use of emerging digital technologies. We also began to develop a comprehensive events and exhibitions programme – quite a departure for a parliament.

And, having reviewed the different administrations, the 2014 independence referendum and the additional powers and responsibilities brought to Holyrood by the Scotland Acts of 2012 and 2016, he wrote:

The key point in this for me is the way the Parliament was able to adapt – and is still adapting – to these substantial changes. We have acquired the confidence that, perhaps, was missing in the early days, simply to get on and make the changes. The parliamentary service, I hope, typifies this – I very rarely hear from my colleagues 'can we do this?' rather 'how will we do this?'

Such flexibility, and willingness to find solutions where new circumstances require them, will be crucial to the future credibility both of the Parliament and of Scottish Governments.

The mind of Donald Dewar was steeped in literature and his address at the opening of the new Parliament in 1999 reflected that cultural depth. He referred to both Robert Burns and Walter Scott, but in the context of a broader set of voices:

> This is about more than our politics and our law. This is about who we are, how we carry ourselves. In the quiet moments today, we might hear some echoes from the past: the shout of the welder in the din of the great Clyde shipyards; the speak of the Mearns, with its soul in the land; the discourse of the enlightenment, when Edinburgh and Glasgow were a light held to the intellectual life of Europe; the wild cry of the great pipes; and back to the distant cries of the battles of Bruce and Wallace.

'Walter Scott,' he continued,

> wrote that only a man with soul so dead could have no sense, no feel of his native land. For me, for any Scot, today is a proud moment; a new stage on a journey begun long ago and which has no end. This is a proud day for all of us.

Sheena Wellington had already sung Burns' 'A Man's a Man for A' That' and a poem by Iain Crichton Smith had been read. Five years later, when the new building was opened at Holyrood, Sheena sang 'A Man's a Man' again, and a poem by the then national Makar, Edwin Morgan, was read out by his friend Liz Lochhead. Literature – the sung, the spoken, the written – was as integral to these political ceremonies as it so often is to the ceremonies of private lives – birthdays, weddings, anniversaries, funerals. Literature that grows from a particular place or culture contains a set of identifying markers, and one of its functions is to articulate – in voices we recognise as our own – hope and complaint, gratitude and intent, praise and criticism; to speak of what unites us and what divides us, of love and loss, of truth and principle.

The achievements and failures of politics and politicians as they happen in and around Parliament are of course significant: they are the daily and weekly news of how our public life is conducted. When unusual things happen, and especially when things go wrong, the news hots up. But any meaningful assessment of the first 20 years of this Parliament's life must have a perspective beyond that period; it must, as Donald Dewar did, look back to the past and forward to the future. I tried to capture this sense of something greater than the immediate in the set of sonnets I wrote when, for three brief days in November 2004, I was 'writer-in-residence' in the new building:

> Under the massive beams and banks of lights
> the oak and sycamore's pale, sweeping grace
> gives a grove-like quality to the place
> as, outside, the afternoon fills with night's
> dark ink. In the gallery a school group
> quietly leaves. Others (young and old) sit
> listening to the debate below. As it
> begins to wind up, the MSPs troop
> in, take their seats. Something ancient and weird
> is in this tribal play, as if instinct
> and ritual have combined, free will and rote;
> as if we all have somehow reappeared
> after long sleep, to find ourselves still linked
> to the thought, to the process, to the vote.
>
> (*Voyage of Intent*, 'The Debating Chamber')

And, paraphrasing some comments made by Enric Miralles, Holyrood's Catalan architect who, like Donald Dewar, did not live to see his work completed, I posited that the steel, wood and concrete structure of the Parliament was less important than the intangible ideas it contained and represented:

> For in the end a Parliament is not
> a building, but a voyage of intent,
> a journey to whatever we might be.
> This is our new departure, this is what
> we opted for, solid and permanent,
> yet tenuous with possibility.
>
> (*Voyage of Intent*, 'The Voyage')

I remember somebody querying that word 'tenuous' in the last line. Was that really what I meant - slender, fragile, doubtful? Yes, it was. 'We' had opted for something definite and real, and there was no doubt about *that*. But where we were heading, how we might guide the vessel and how in turn the journey might shape us - all that was unknown and uncertain. There are no guarantees against storm, piracy or even shipwreck. Nevertheless, as Robert Louis Stevenson once wrote:

> Who, if he were wisely considerate of things at large, would ever embark upon any work much more considerable than a halfpenny postcard?

There is little doubt that, since the referendum of 2014, any sense of the 'process' of devolution is linked to questions about independence and Scotland's longer-term relationship with the other constituent parts of the United Kingdom, with the EU and with the wider world. Yet if it is not clear what devolution may look like in another 20 years, nor is it easy to say exactly what independence would look like if it came about. It seems to me, therefore, that whatever Scotland's constitutional destination, many of the same issues will have to be addressed by the Parliament as part of a wider conversation about what kind of society people want to live in.

Those issues are of course not unique to Scotland. There will have to be robust, open and inclusive discussions about health, welfare, education, housing, employment and what level of services people need or should expect and how to deliver and pay for them. We will have to ask what kind of economy is likely to give us stability, sustainability and an acceptable standard of living for all, what the environmental impact of our choices will be and how we will create and manage our energy supplies. These questions beg others about land ownership, income equality, forms of taxation and the relationship between the public and private sectors. We will have to ask whether we should measure our social and economic health by financial statistics or happiness statistics or by what combination of both.

The Parliament itself, while never losing sight of these vital political matters, will have to build a framework for debating them. Should there be further electoral reform? Should there be further dispersal of power from Edinburgh to the regions and islands of this diverse country, and how might that be done so that local people are genuinely empowered? Should there be a written Scottish constitution? Could there be such a thing in one part of the UK but not in another? And what principles would be laid down in such a document, that might borrow from the constitutions of other countries or perhaps be more progressive and far-reaching than theirs? Even to consider a written constitution raises fundamental questions about, for example, the monarchy, the relationship between law-makers and law-enforcers, the tricky balance between individual rights and societal responsibilities. Who knows how these questions will be resolved, but the prospect of having such discussions here, on our own turf and in our own terms, is an invigorating one, a prospect that we should welcome as our politics and our political institutions, especially our Parliament, matures in the coming decades - without, it is to be hoped, becoming staid or stultified or self-reverential.

I began with one fictional reflection on parliamentary function and will end with another. In a passage from my novel *And the Land Lay Still* (2010) one of the characters, Mike Pendreich, is reflecting on the involvement of himself and his friend Jean Barbour in the long campaign for a Scottish Parliament. The year is 2008, so already nearly a decade has passed since the Parliament was established:

> *My contribution to the cause*: Jean's words. But what was the cause? It's easy to remember what they stood *against*: Thatcherism, London rule, the destruction of old industries, the assault on the Welfare State, the poll tax. But what were they *for*? A Scottish parliament, of course. But now they have it, what is *it* for? Forget smoking bans and other worthwhile legislation, what is its primary function? Maybe it's for saying, *Look, listen, this is who we are*. And maybe that is no insignificant thing, and the purpose of a parliament is to say it again, over and over. What can be more important, politically, than to know who you are, and to say it?

# The Scottish Parliament in a Changing World

JIM JOHNSTON AND JAMES MITCHELL

## Living in the Shadow of 1979

POLITICAL WATERSHEDS ARE generally evident only well after they have occurred, but 1979 was recognised to be a watershed moment in Scottish and UK politics at the time. Prime Minister Callaghan reflected on the changes he discerned in the closing stages of his premiership:

> You know there are times, perhaps once every 30 years, when there is a sea-change in politics. It then does not matter what you say or what you do. There is a shift in what the public wants and what it approves of.

There was little doubt that politics was about to change though few, including his successor herself, could have anticipated the changes to come. Very different changes had been anticipated only a few years, even months, before this in Scotland. Supporters of a Scottish Assembly had been preparing for a new constitutional order and the opportunities it would offer, focusing on policies to be pursued by a Scottish Assembly. But they had over-estimated support for their cause and the policy-wonking had been in vain.

The combination of the disappointing referendum results and the election of a government hostile to devolution were described in an article by Neal Ascherson in *The Scotsman* in November that year:

> This round of Scottish politics is over. There will be another. Too much points that way to be wrong: the irrevocable experience and preparations of the seventies; the continuing decline of the British economy and the way this Government makes the outlying parts of the UK pay most dearly for that decline; the more general decay of the British state and its unreformed institutions; the lack of purpose in the Labour movement;

the relentless pressure on Scotland through the eighties of the European Community – where we have no special voice for our special interests.

The post-referendum period was one of introspection and the finger of blame was pointed across and within parties that had campaigned for the assembly. Scottish politics lived in the shadow of 1979 for the next two decades. There would be another round. Scottish politics since the Treaty of Union has been a succession of rounds. The question of Scotland's place in the UK has been and never can be 'settled'. Each generation has had to consider afresh Scotland's relations with its neighbours.

Thomas Jefferson understood this well and advocated for what we would call inter-generational justice. He argued that 'no society can make a perpetual constitution, or even a perpetual law'. The Jeffersonian view was that no generation should dictate terms or policies to generations unborn. Constitution-makers, MSPs and citizens alive at any point in time are stewards with no right to impose obligations on future generations. By chance, Jefferson's view that constitutions needed to be reviewed every 19 years or so was essentially what happened following the 1979 referendum. By 1997, there had been a sea-change in public opinion. It had not taken 30 years, as Jim Callaghan had speculated. There was a depth and urgency in support that was absent in 1979. It had become associated with a clearer sense of devolution's purpose while simultaneously lacking in a programme for government. Supporters of devolution knew what they were against but less what they supported. The Scottish Parliament would be a defensive measure, a means of blocking unpopular policies coming from Westminster. The campaign in 1997 was more cautious than that in 1997. Campaigning in the shadow of 1979 meant that more effort was made to build consensus and cross-party support.

The 1997 referendum allowed supporters of a legislature to finally emerge from the shadow of the 1979 referendum. But it was a Parliament whose members had given scant attention to what it might actually do. It did not matter which party or parties had won in 1999, there was a policy deficit to replace the 'democratic deficit' that some saw as its purpose to fill. Coincidentally, there was no shortage of public money in the first two terms of the Parliament which removed the perceived need to be innovative and imaginative in policy development. An emphasis on policy divergence animated commentators and many parliamentarians, reflecting the defensive logic of devolution.

Devolved government had been conceived as a kind of dual polity in which Scotland would be cocooned from UK decisions that a majority in Scotland opposed. But devolved government could never entirely work like that. No amount of legalistic jurisdictional boundary definitions can ever overcome public policy overlaps and spill overs. High walls might make good neighbours but, as the experience of the Brexit debates have demonstrated, are not a realistic option when it comes to relations between neighbouring polities. Scotland will be affected by decisions in London even if Scotland is independent, just as Westminster will not free itself from decisions made in Brussels after Brexit. But that did not mean that Scotland had no autonomy, only that autonomy is relative.

But what did Scotland do with the relative autonomy it had which coincided with public financial good times? First and foremost, it did what the public wanted and poured money into selective public services. It did, as anticipated, refuse to follow London in many, though by no means all, policy innovations which were deemed to follow a 'neo-liberal' course. But mostly what was striking was what the Parliament failed to do. It is ironic that the Biblical warning that seven years of great plenty would be followed by seven years of famine was ignored given that meetings were held in the Kirk's General Assembly Hall in the early years. But, as spin replaced policy analysis, the mantra of the moment was that boom and bust had ended.

Jeffersonian notions of stewardship and inter-generational justice were ignored on the assumption of onwards and upwards public spending. Scotland was perhaps no different from elsewhere. 'Dead men rule' across the globe as is often noted in the US meaning that policies determined in the past (mainly by men) continue in place well after they were first enunciated, and continue to impact on resources and, in many instances, at the same time as demand is increasing. Expanding public commitments without regard to expanding costs and limited sources of funding are plaguing policy making. There was little attention to the implications of the long-term effects of policy decisions made in the good years.

It has proved easier to address the immediate needs and desires of those most engaged, those most likely to vote. There is little incentive to consider future generations. This is privately acknowledged by politicians across the Parliament who make the reasonable observation that it would be electorally difficult, though much stronger language is often used, to redistribute resources today to benefit unborn voters at the expense of those most likely to turn out next time round. One of the key challenges over the next 20 years will be to find ways that make it possible to embed Jeffersonian notions of stewardship and inter-generational justice in the Scottish Parliament.

## Where Are We Now?

The 20th anniversary of devolution provides an opportunity for the Scottish Parliament to take stock of how far it has travelled in a relatively short period of time. All of our authors have provided thoughtful reflections on what has been achieved by the young Parliament, where it has been less successful and the challenges and opportunities that it is likely to face in the next 20 years.

In our introduction we highlight that a parliament has three main functions. Our authors are generally positive about the way in which Holyrood has carried out these functions but there is also clearly more that can be done.

In relation to policy-making, Bernard Ponsonby points out that while the Parliament has not been afraid to make different policy choices from Westminster, the culture is curiously conservative and that all of the parties have taken a safety-first approach to policy. Similarly, David Eiser and Graeme Roy highlight, in relation to economic and fiscal challenges, that policy looks remarkably similar now as it did in 1999 and that, on the big tax issues, the Parliament has shied away from bold reform.

A failure to tackle high levels of poverty is emphasised as one of the main policy failures of devolution – though the extent to which the Parliament had sufficient powers to make much of a difference has to be acknowledged. Bernard suggests that lifting the marginalised from the fringes of our society to equip them to enjoy what most of us take for granted is the biggest challenge facing the Parliament. Graeme Roy and David Eiser point out that for all the talk of 'inclusive growth' nearly one million people, including nearly one in four children, live in poverty.

Demographic change and an ageing society is another policy area which is emphasised here as a major challenge for the Parliament. Bernard Ponsonby believes that the key hurdle to jump will be to sustain and improve the provision of public services which will be tested to the breaking point by a series of demographic factors. Graeme Roy and David Eiser stress the profound effect which demographic change will have on the Scottish economy and the public finances over the next 20 years. Alan Convery and David Parker write that this will inlcude how to pay for generous pension and healthcare provisions with fewer workers to contribute and that the Parliament will need to resolve this difficult cross-generational challenge. But we must not ignore the fact that people growing older is a cause for celebration and that Scottish society is served well by the immense, un-der-valued contributions of many older people. We should take heed of the words of World Health Organisation's Margaret Chan:

> Older people are a wonderful resource for their families and communities, and in the formal or informal workforce. They are a repository of knowl-edge. They can help us avoid making the same mistakes again.

Caroline Gardner reminds us that while many of the challenges which the Parliament faces are often complex, policy solutions can be much simpler, for example, through listening more closely to the everyday frustrations of our street level third sector volunteers and public service professionals and the solutions they propose. As Talat Yaqoob highlights this means the Parliament needs to

> hear more and directly from the social care worker, the single parent, the immigrant, the nurse or the cleaner.

A key theme which runs through a number of the chapters is the ex-tent to which the Parliament has succeeded in linking the people and law-makers. Talat Yaqoob writes that there is no denying that the par-ticipatory culture within the Scottish Parliament differs from that of Westminster and the level of access and public engagement is lauded as one of the signature ways in which Scottish politics works. But there is more to be done and new challenges and opportunities will arise espe-cially with changes in technology.

Laura Beveridge and Rosie Moore remind us of the possibilities which a parliamentary democracy provides. Laura writes of her role in the 1000 Voices campaign and being welcomed into the Parliament as an unforget-table experience. She firmly believes that it is a place for all of us. Rosie writes about her experience of giving evidence on behalf of the Independ-ent Care Review to the Education and Skills Committee. She describes it as very empowering and that she was genuinely being listened to.

Moving forward a key challenge, as underscored by Alison Evison, is the relationship between central government and local democracy. The vitality that exists in our communities has not been harnessed as effectively as it might over the last 20 years. Similarly, Gillian Baxendine believes that the Parliament needs to be unafraid to talk openly about the tensions between the representative democracy of the past and the growing demand for participation and how we can experiment with blending the two. Fiona Duncan reminds us that trust is fragile and once lost is very difficult to earn back, and so politicians should seek to authentically interact with the people they are representing and avoid exploitative and tokenistic methods of engagement.

A number of our contributors emphasise the opportunities which digital technology provides in reimagining how our elected politicians engage with the people they represent. From a local government perspective, Alison points out the Parliament cannot deliver higher levels of participation on its own and that both would benefit from sharing and learning from each other. Citizens' juries and other forms of deliberative democracy as well as participative budgeting are some examples provided by our contributors as options for delivering a more participative democracy.

A further challenge is the extent to which the Parliament has effectively engaged with the business community. Michael Crow points out that the relationship between business and parliament has not been as strong as it could have been. His view is that parliament and business have never managed to find a way of working well enough together to find solutions to the issues of the day, evaluate what policies work and what don't and implement a long-term business strategy for Scotland. Michael believes that this failure by both business and parliament to develop a strong relationship over the last 20 years must be addressed and is imperative that parliament and business collaborates.

The effectiveness of the Parliament's relationship with local government is also raised by some of our contributors. In particular, whether the promise that relations between the Parliament and local government would be based on mutual respect and parity of esteem have been realised. This is based on an acceptance that local government, as the only other elected authority, has a legitimacy that matched that of the Scottish Parliament. But Alison Evison's view is it is difficult to avoid the disappointment felt across local government that such high ideals have been lost. She suggests that the 20th anniversary provides an opportunity to assess progress, consider challenges that lie ahead and discuss how to re-imagine how these ideals and principles should be translated into practice. Jim Wallace agrees. He suggests that the extent to which Parliament can rise to the challenge of reforming local government finance and revitalising democracy should be a measure of its success in its third decade.

## Always Something Unexpected Around the Corner

It is now commonly asserted that the only thing that is certain is uncertainty. There is little doubt that this creates frustrations and discontent, making politics much less predictable. It contributes to a rise of populism. Scotland cannot expect to be immune so long as this current turbulence continues. The Parliament's experience of multi-party politics has been relatively limited. The parties that have gained seats at each successive election can make no assumptions about the future. As the electorate become less rooted, each election must be fought as if facing an entirely new electorate. Fewer and fewer voters may feel any party loyalty and parties will have to work harder for our support. Scotland's electoral system makes this more likely to be manifest in Holyrood. The Commons' electoral system creates a much higher barrier for entry so at one level we might expect to see more new faces and parties.

Yet, the opportunities that an entirely new Parliament offered are unlikely to occur again. Holyrood has consistently returned more women than the Commons because it was a new institution lacking the drag that an existing parliament carries with it. Further change will likely be slow without some disruption. Holyrood can take some pride in its early years but there is no more conservative institution than one that's pride is based only on its past achievements. The issue of representation is only the Parliamentary manifestation of wider societal challenges. A key question is the extent to which changes in representation affect society. It is difficult to know how a future of turbulent politics might play out in terms of different forms of representation.

And we must ask how changing representation can be made to help people outside Parliament. Has reducing the voting age to 16 made much difference in terms of inter-generational justice? Are 16 and 17 year olds any better represented in Parliament? This is not an argument against Votes at 16, but a question of how to ensure that the voices and interests of those 16 and 17 year olds are truly found voice in our decision-making processes. As Alan Convery and David Parker suggest:

> The fundamental challenge facing representative democracy is that cost burdens rest most heavily on future generations that do not yet have the franchise. Extending the right of 16 and 17-year-olds to vote in Scottish Parliamentary elections is one key step not only because of this inter-generation resource imbalance but also to attempt to spur increased interest in the Scottish Government and its affairs at an earlier age.

## The Unanswerable Scottish Question

Scotland's constitutional status can never be 'solved'. There can be no settled will of the people because we can never know what tomorrow's people will want. We return to Jefferson. He argued that no constitution should exist in perpetuity. Dead men should not rule generations not yet born in determining constitutional arrangements or everyday public policy. By his calculation, a new constitution was required every 19 years. But there will be implications for the Parliament whatever answers are offered. Devolution is currently undergoing change. The Parliament that met for the first time 20 years ago required skills and resources that are now insufficient. This does not mean that MSPs should be experts in areas now devolved but that sufficient Parliamentary resources are at their disposal to allow them to engage effectively.

Scottish Parliamentarians took justifiable pride in creating a more modern legislature compared with Westminster. In many respects, Holyrood was envisaged as different kind of Parliament. But over the last 20 years, reforms in the House of Commons suggest that, in important respects, the Commons has overtaken Holyrood in becoming the more modern institution. While the Commons may retain many features of ancient (albeit often invented) traditions with time-consuming votes involving members traipsing through lobbies, the Scottish Parliament could learn much from its committee system. Elected conveners, relatively well-resourced committees and more time to devote to both scrutinising government and legislation make the Commons a different body from that which existed two decades ago. In one crucial respect, both bodies are similar, each belonging to the same 'family' of legislatures. Neither Holyrood nor Westminster are policy-making bodies in the way that some legislatures are, but both are executive-dominated. The Scottish Parliament has contributed much in terms of legitimacy, it has had an impact in terms of the linkage with the people and contributed to scrutinising the Scottish Government. But it has still to realise a significant role in policy initiation and policy-making.

While this book has shown that there is a lively debate about the future role of the Parliament there is little, if any, debate about its legitimacy as a representative body. It has established itself as a permanent feature within Scotland's political landscape. In one respect this permanence is a consequence of the building itself which has quickly become recognisable as an iconic symbol of modern Scotland. While governments come and go and some MSPs are re-elected or not, the building remains as a physical reminder of the strength of the political system which made it possible in the first place. But as James Robertson points out, the steel, wood and concrete structure of the Parliament is less important than the intangible ideas it contains and represents –

> For in the end a Parliament is not
> a building, but a voyage of intent,
> a journey to whatever we might be.

# Appendix

## A Users' Guide to the Scottish Parliament

ELIZABETH CANTLIE AND ANDREW AITON

THE SCOTTISH PARLIAMENT works on behalf of all the people of Scotland, wherever they live and whatever language they use. It does this by debating issues, holding inquiries, examining proposals for new laws, reviewing the effectiveness of existing laws and questioning Scottish Government ministers and other decision-makers. Your views and experiences are important to the work of the Scottish Parliament. Below is some information on how you can let us know what matters to you.

### Contact your MSPs

Each person in Scotland is represented by *eight* members of the Scottish Parliament (MSPs). Your MSPs all have the same status and you can contact any of the eight who represent you in any language. You can contact an MSP even if you didn't vote for them. You can contact them by phone, email, letter or through social media. MSPs may also hold surgeries in their local area to give you an opportunity to meet them and discuss matters of concern in person.

MSPs can: lodge a motion to get support for an issue; speak in a debate; ask a question of Scottish Government ministers; refer matters to, or ask a question of, another person or organisation such as a council or a health board; introduce a bill to change the law; propose changes to a current bill.

### Get Involved in the Work of Committees

Committees are small groups of MSPs who look at specific subjects such as health, the economy or justice. Each committee is chaired by a convener and most of the current committees have seven or nine MSPs as members.

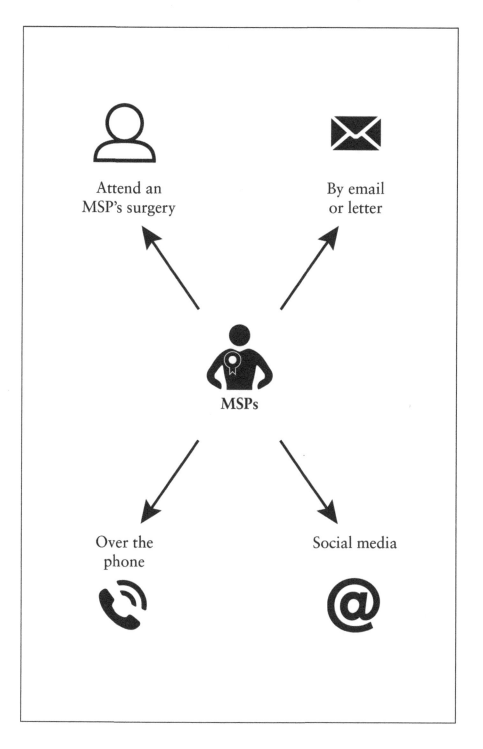

Members reflect the balance of the various political parties and groupings in the Scottish Parliament.

Committees invite members of the public to give their views on the issues they are considering. They can also invite any person to attend a meeting as a witness. Witnesses give evidence related to the business of the committee.

Committees aim to involve as many people as possible in the democratic process. By giving your views to a committee, you may influence legislation or the policies of the Scottish Government.

You can write to a committee or submit a video in response to a call for evidence on an inquiry or a bill. You can also attend committee events, complete a survey or interact with most committees through social media.

## Submit or Support a Public Petition

You can submit or support a public petition asking the Scottish Parliament to look into a matter of national public interest or concern, to change existing laws or to introduce new laws.

You need only *one* signature for your petition to be considered.

You can raise a petition online to attract a wider audience. You can also give your views on online petitions or add your signature to show your support.

## Other Ways to Engage

### Cross-Party Groups

Joining a cross-party group (CPG) will enable you to meet with MSPs and other individuals and organisations who share the same interest in a particular cause or subject.

To join or attend a meeting of a CPG, you should approach the group contact directly. A list of all CPGs, including their members and contact details, is available on the Scottish Parliament website.

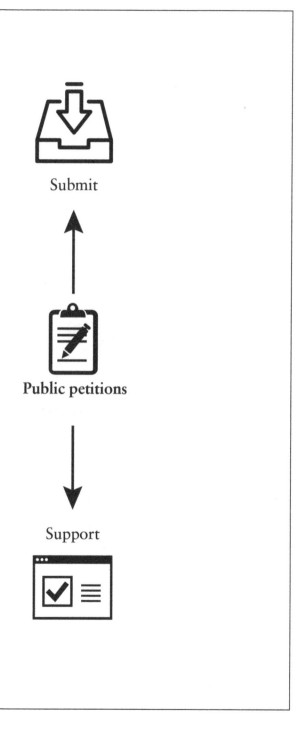

Submit

Public petitions

Support

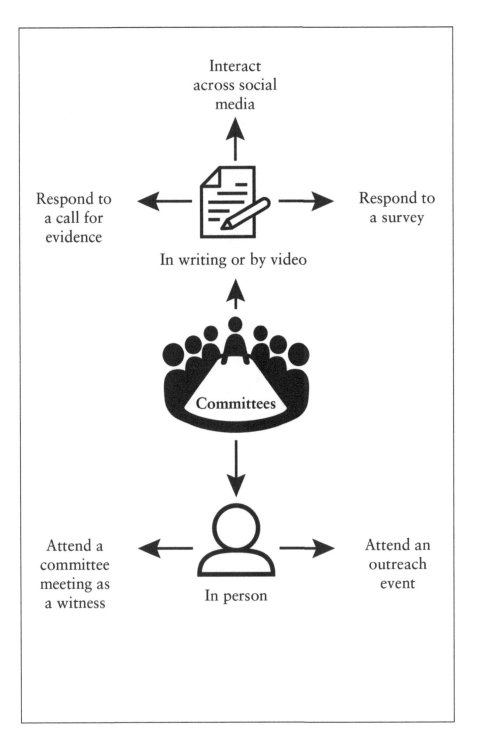

## *Events and Exhibitions*

The Scottish Parliament hosts a wide range of events and exhibitions, including those with a direct link to the work of parliamentary committees and those sponsored by MSPs.

Events may also be held to mark a particular occasion such as the start of a new parliamentary session.

With the sponsorship of an MSP, you can hold an event or exhibition to raise awareness of a particular issue related to the work of the Parliament.

## *How to Contact the Scottish Parliament*

Key ways for you to make your views known to the Scottish Parliament on issues you care about. If you want to find out more about the Scottish Parliament, there are lots of ways to get in touch:

Telephone: 0800 092 7500 / 0131 348 5000
0131 348 5395 (*Gàidhlig*)

Calls are also welcome using the Text Relay service or in British Sign Language (BSL) through contactscotland-bsl.org

Email: info@parliament.scot
Live chat: parliament.scot/live-chat
Address: Public Information and Resources
The Scottish Parliament
Edinburgh EH99 1SP

Facebook: /scottishparliament
parliament.scot/bsl-facebook-group (for BSL users)
Instagram: /scotparl/
Twitter: @scotparl
@parlalba (*Gàidhlig*)
YouTube: /ScottishParliament

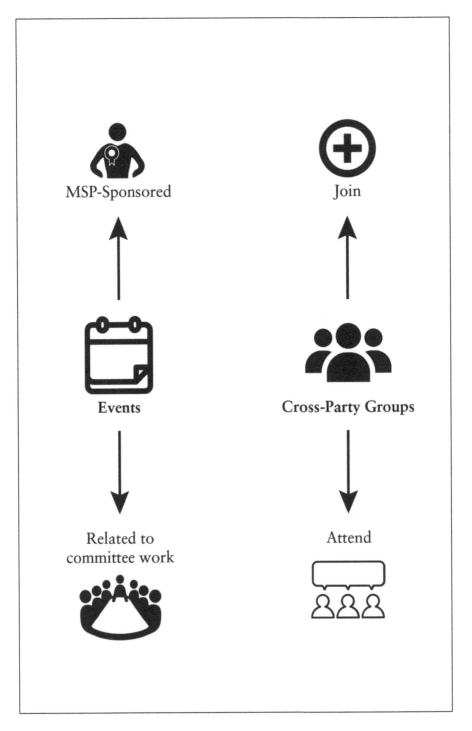

The Parliament's website contains information in a range of languages, and our Gaelic Language Plan and British Sign Language Plan tell you how we are supporting and developing Gaelic and BSL in the Scottish Parliament. We are continually developing new ways of providing information and of enabling the public to get involved in the work of the Parliament, and your feedback on these is always welcome.

# Contributor Biographies

ANDREW AITON is the Data Visualisation Manager, in the Scottish Parliament Information Centre (SPICe). He is responsible for producing and overseeing the data visualisation work of SPICe and the Scottish Parliament's committees. Previously he was the Data Manager within SPICe, where he worked at improving data visualisation and promoting its use throughout the Parliament.

CHARLOTTE BARBOUR has worked for the Institute of Chartered Accountants of Scotland for many years in a range of policy and regulatory roles. For the last five years, she has supported the ICAS Tax Board, which has overall responsibility for all tax matters affecting ICAS members and oversight of five technical committees responsible for Scottish taxes, private client taxes, international taxes, indirect taxes and small business taxes. She has extensive experience in dealing with tax issues and has represented ICAS at both the Scottish Parliament and the House of Lords, and regularly speaks on both radio and TV. Charlotte is the author of the Bloomsbury book entitled *The Management of Taxes in Scotland*.

GILLIAN BAXENDINE was brought up in Edinburgh (in fact her father worked for Scottish & Newcastle Breweries on the site where the Scottish Parliament now stands). After several years working for the Civil Service in London, she returned to Edinburgh as one of the first clerk team leaders appointed to the Scottish Parliamentary Service. Her first role at the Parliament was to organise the 1999 Opening Ceremony and she was then clerk to various parliamentary committees, including Education, Justice & Standards & Procedures. In 2018, she was appointed as head of the newly established committee engagement unit, supporting committees to involve a wider range of people in their work and trying out new ways for people to participate.

LEE BRIDGES has worked in a parliamentary environment for 20 years. In 1999, he joined the staff of the new Scottish Parliament and in his ten years there worked in committees, the chamber and as Principal Private Secretary to the Presiding Officer. He joined the House of Commons in 2010 and led the Savings Programme before becoming the Speaker's Press Secretary between 2012 and 2014. He was the House's Director of Communications between 2014 and June 2018. He has been the Senior Responsible Owner of the Independent Complaints and Grievance Scheme since April 2018, leading the team of officials who have drawn up and implemented the scheme.

ELIZABETH CANTLIE (MA Hons, PhD) is the Public Information Supervisor and has worked in the Parliament since 1999.

SARAH CHILDS is Professor of Politics and Gender at Birkbeck, University of London. Her research expertise centres on the theory and practice of women's representation, gender and political parties, and re-gendering parliaments. Sarah is writing a book *Feminist Democrat Representation*, with Karen Celis. She has received the Political Studies Association 'Special Recognition Award' in 2015. 2016 saw the publication of 'The Good Parliament Report' following a secondment to the UK House of Commons. On Sarah's recommendation a new group of MPs, The Commons Reference Group on Representation and Inclusion was established by Mr Speaker. Sarah is currently advising this group.

ALAN CONVERY is a senior lecturer in politics at the University of Edinburgh. He received his PhD from Strathclyde University in 2014. He works on British and Scottish politics and conservatism and the Conservative Party. His first book, *The Territorial Conservative Party: Devolution and Party Change in Scotland and Wales*, was published by Manchester University Press in 2016.

MICHAEL CROW is Head of Public Affairs for RBS Group and a member of the bank's Scotland Board. His background is in politics and journalism. From 1997 to 1999 he was Westminster Correspondent for STV covering the 1997 general election, the devolution referendum and the Scotland Act. He then returned to Scotland in 1999 to cover the opening and establishment of the Scottish Parliament. Michael worked as STV's Political Correspondent until 2009 and also presented a number of the station's programmes, both political and non-political. He then moved to the Conservative Party as Director of Strategy and Communications in Scotland before joining RBS in 2010.

FIONA DUNCAN is the CEO of the Corra Foundation and has over 25 years' experience working in the voluntary sector in Scotland and overseas. Prior to joining the Foundation, Fiona worked as a consultant dedicated to not-for-profits, and held roles at Capability Scotland, the Royal Scottish Academy of Music and Drama and WaterAid. Fiona is also Chair of the Independent Care Review which will report on making change happen for children and young people who experience what is known as the 'care system' in 2020. In 2018 Fiona was awarded the Saltire Award for her contribution to Scottish Public Life.

DAVID EISER is a research fellow at the Fraser of Allander Institute at the University of Strathclyde, specialising in Scottish fiscal policy and the Scottish budget. He has been an adviser to the Scottish Parliament's Finance and Constitution Committee since 2016.

CLLR ALISON EVISON is the 15th President of the Convention of Scottish Local Authorities. She was first elected to Aberdeenshire Council in 2012 and served as co-leader of the Council for a period. She was a teacher before being elected to the council and retains a keen interest in education.

CAROLINE GARDNER has been the Auditor General for Scotland since 2012, responsible for auditing the Scottish Government and public bodies in Scotland and reporting to the Scottish Parliament. She has 30 years' experience in audit, governance and financial management, and is the accountable officer for Audit Scotland. A qualified accountant and Fellow of the Chartered Institute of Public Finance and Accountancy (CIPFA), where she served as President 2006–07. Caroline has an MBA from Warwick Business School, is a Fellow of the Royal Society of Edinburgh and has been a Director of Public Sector Audit Appointments Ltd since 2014.

JIM JOHNSTON has been a clerk in the Scottish Parliament since 1999, including a period on secondment to the House of Lords, and previously received a PhD in Political Science from the University of Birmingham.

MOIRA KELLY has recently retired from a long career in tax, working in professional practice. She is a member of Council of the Chartered Institute of Taxation and has just stood down as chair of the Institute's Scottish technical committee.

JAMES MITCHELL is professor of Public Policy at the University of Edinburgh. He has written extensively on Scottish and UK politics and public policy.

CHRISTINE O'NEILL is Chairman of Brodies LLP. She is a recognised expert in constitutional and administrative law and is co-author, with Professor Chris Himsworth, of *Scotland's Constitution: Law and Practice*. Christine has been an external adviser to the Scottish Parliament's Devolution (Further Powers) Committee and its Finance and Constitution Committee. In her capacity as a solicitor advocate she is currently First Standing Junior to the Scottish Government, representing the Government in litigation. She was part of the Lord Advocate's legal team in the Supreme Court in the Gina Miller case and in the defence of the challenge to the UK Withdrawal from the European Union (Legal Continuity) (Scotland) Bill.

DAVID PARKER is an associate professor of Political Science at Montana State University. He studies legislatures, with a particular focus on how legislators craft representational styles as well as the process of legislative oversight. He is the author of *Battle for the Big Sky: Representation and the Politics of Place in the Race for the U.S. Senate* (CQ Press) and *The Power of Money in Congressional Campaigns, 1880–2006* (University of Oklahoma Press). His published research on the Scottish Parliament examines the consequences of the mixed-member proportional electoral system on whether and how MSPs build a personal vote and how partisan branding dominates MSP willingness to participate in First Minister's Questions and the type of questions they ask. Parker provides frequent media commentary for local state and national news outlets on American and British politics, including the *Washington Post*, *The New York Times*, NPR's *Morning Edition*, PBS's *Frontline*, and the Sundance award-winning documentary *Dark Money*.

BERNARD PONSONBY is the special correspondent for STV News, having served as the station's political editor for nearly 19 years. He has reported from Holyrood, Westminster and Brussels and has been the principal presenter of all election, by-election, referendum and election results programmes for the last 25 years. He was awarded the Royal Television Society (Scotland) Journalist of the year for two successive years in 2015 and 2016. Bernard has interviewed five Prime Ministers and all of Scotland's First Ministers.

CHARLES ROBERT was appointed Clerk of the House of Commons of Canada in July 2017, having previously served as the Clerk of the Senate and Clerk of the Parliaments. He has served on the Editorial Board of the *Canadian Parliamentary Review* since 1998 and is a member of the Canadian Association of Clerks at the Table, the Association of Secretaries General of Parliament and the Association des secrétaires généraux des parlements francophones. He has also written a number of articles on procedure including several on parliamentary privilege that have appeared in *The Table* and the *Canadian Parliamentary Review.*

JAMES ROBERTSON is a poet, writer of fiction and editor. His novels include *The Testament of Gideon Mack* (long-listed for the Booker Prize), *Joseph Knight* and *And the Land Lay Still* (both Saltire Society Scottish Books of the Year), and he has published four books of short stories, several poetry collections and works of non-fiction, most recently *Arrest This Moment*, a biography of the Dundee songwriter Michael Marra. He also co-founded Itchy Coo, an imprint specialising in books in Scots for young readers and is its general editor as well as a contributing author and translator. For three days in November 2004, he was writer-in-residence at the Scottish Parliament's newly-opened building.

GRAEME ROY is professor of economics and, since 2016, director of the Fraser of Allander Institute at the University of Strathclyde. He was previously head of the First Minister's policy unit at the Scottish Government.

LORD WALLACE OF TANKERNESS is a Liberal Democrat peer in the House of Lords. As Jim Wallace, he was MP for Orkney and Shetland from 1983–2001 and MSP for Orkney from 1999–2007. He led the Scottish Liberal Democrats from 1992 to 2005 and, on the creation of the Scottish Parliament, became Deputy First

Minister and Minister for Justice and, later, Minister for Enterprise & Lifelong Learning. He also took the role of acting First Minister. As a member of the House of Lords, he was Advocate General for Scotland from 2010 to 2015 in the UK coalition government. He led the Lib Dem peers from 2013 to 2016 and was deputy leader of the House of Lords from 2013 to 2015. He became a Queen's Counsel in 1997, a privy councillor in 2000 and was elected a fellow of the Royal Society of Edinburgh in 2018.

TALAT YAQOOB is a feminist and equalities campaigner. She has a background in third sector project management, campaign development and public affairs. Her work focuses on women's economic and political inequality and intersectionality in policy-making. She has campaigned on a range of issues including women's political representation, women's participation in STEM, inequality across further and higher education, race equality and Muslim women's equality.

# **Luath** Press Limited

*committed to publishing well written books worth reading*

LUATH PRESS takes its name from Robert Burns, whose little collie Luath (*Gael.*, swift or nimble) tripped up Jean Armour at a wedding and gave him the chance to speak to the woman who was to be his wife and the abiding love of his life. Burns called one of the 'Twa Dogs' Luath after Cuchullin's hunting dog in Ossian's *Fingal*. Luath Press was established in 1981 in the heart of Burns country, and is now based a few steps up the road from Burns' first lodgings on Edinburgh's Royal Mile. Luath offers you distinctive writing with a hint of unexpected pleasures.

Most bookshops in the UK, the US, Canada, Australia, New Zealand and parts of Europe, either carry our books in stock or can order them for you. To order direct from us, please send a £sterling cheque, postal order, international money order or your credit card details (number, address of cardholder and expiry date) to us at the address below. Please add post and packing as follows: UK – £1.00 per delivery address; overseas surface mail – £2.50 per delivery address; overseas airmail – £3.50 for the first book to each delivery address, plus £1.00 for each additional book by airmail to the same address. If your order is a gift, we will happily enclose your card or message at no extra charge.

**Luath** Press Limited
543/2 Castlehill
The Royal Mile
Edinburgh EH1 2ND
Scotland
Telephone: +44 (0)131 225 4326 (24 hours)
email: sales@luath. co.uk
Website: www. luath.co.uk